MY BROTHER'S BICYCLE

LES STANLEY

A catalogue record for this book is available from the National Library
of Australia

Paperback
ISBN-13: 978-0-6481892-6-8

E-Book
ISBN-13: 978-0-6481892-7-5

Editor: Desolie Page (AE)
Cover Design by c8v_logos on Fiverr
Internal formatting by Lisa Hannan Fox

Photo on cover taken at Théoule-sur-Mer, France by author's wife

Photo on page 5 taken in Enfield, England in 1976 just before original
departure

CONTENTS

Prologue   1
Introduction   3

1976

Used Cars   9
The East Ender   11
Long Hot Summer   14
Down to Kent   16
What's a Hovercraft?   18
Honeymoon Night   20
Toilets and Henry   22
Shopping for Spares   24
Italian Lifts   26
More Toilets   28
Rome, the Infernal City   30
Somewhere in Italy   32
Braking (sic) Point   34
Greek Night   36
Homeward Bound   37
Home for a While   41
A Bit About Herne Bay   42

THE YEARS IN BETWEEN

Germany   49
Overland to India   52
London and the Tourist Board   58
6 Months on the Kibbutz   60
Copenhagen   66

Return to India and Australia Trip One	68
Disaster in Dublin	70
The London Depression	73
British Airways	75
Australia Trip Two	80
Return to Europe	82
Bangkok	85
Leaving Bangkok	89
The Final Years in France	92

OTHER JOURNEYS

Commuting – London	97
Commuting – Waltrop, Germany	99
Commuting – Copenhagen	101
Commuting – Brisbane	103
Commuting – Bangkok	104

2018

La Vita Nuova	109
To Camp or Not	111
40+ Years On	113
Delivery and Collection	115
e-commute	117
Extras	119
Across the Border	120
Lyon to Mandelieu – Strike 1	123
Day 1	127
Day 2	129
Day 3	130
Day 4	134
Italy Again	135
Mandelieu to Levanto, Italy	138
San Remo to Albenga	140
Albenga	141

To Genoa and Beyond 144
Rapallo to Monterosso Cinque Terre by Train 146
Girl on a Train 149
Now and Then 151
In Rapallo 154
Rapallo to Deiva Marina 156
Deiva Marina to Levanto 159
Heading Home to Mandelieu by Train 161
Changing Trains in Genoa 163
Tandem Memories 166
Genoa Again 168
Enfield to Herne Bay – 2018 174
Bruce, Henry and Time Manager – Part 1 176
Bruce, Henry and Time Manager – Part 2 182
The Zoco Effect 188
Side Trip to Canterbury 189
Whitstable to Reculver – 2018 192
Ian Robert Stanley 11/07/1950 – 30/01/2015 195
One of Many Endings 197
Final Departure and a New Beginning 203

References 205
Thanks for Reading 207
About Les Stanley 209

PROLOGUE

I had always thought that, when the time came, I would opt for cremation. It seemed more final. I imagined my ashes being blasted into space or scattered across the pool table of The Druid's Head pub, my teenage drinking hole in Herne Bay, Kent. The illegality of such an act seemed somehow fitting and would, in my mind, complete the great circle of life. That was my plan for the time I knew would come eventually.

But, as my brother's incongruously shiny coffin descended into the neatly dug grave, I'd had to admit to myself that maybe burial was the way to go. It seemed so much more dignified than disappearing behind a curtain.

My brother Ian's death had not been a big surprise. A shock, yes. Sad, undoubtedly. He was leaving behind two children still only in their twenties. Too young to lose your dad. But a surprise? Not really. He'd been suffering from a number of ailments for some time and had finally been diagnosed with a serious blood disorder. Looking back on my last few conversations with him I think he knew that time was something he did not have much of.

I had no further opportunity to reminisce. My reverie was interrupted as a large, badly loaded truck, driven, presumably, by an equally large and, in all likelihood, equally loaded, Eastern European, thundered past my left shoulder. I really must find a quieter road, I thought, or my mangled body will need boxing or burning earlier than intended. I took a deep breath and pedalled on looking forward to the first cappuccino of the day.

INTRODUCTION

After my brother passed away I discovered that, just before he became seriously ill, he had purchased an electric bike. Always a fairly keen cyclist he was obviously not going to let a still-to-be-fully diagnosed heart condition stop him from enjoying himself. As his health deteriorated and reached the sad conclusion of his demise and, later, while the complications of a will settlement were ongoing, his shiny new bike languished in his garage. This series of events coincided with my own return to Europe from a lengthy period of living in Asia. I had been living in Bangkok, Thailand, not a city renowned as a cycling paradise. As his younger brother, and a cyclist myself, it seemed fitting that I inherit his machine. It would provide me with a good opportunity to re-acquaint myself with riding.

So I hatched a plan.

Many years previously I had ridden a bike from London to Athens. The reality being that I had partly ridden that route, as much of the journey was eventually completed using other forms of transport. And it wasn't just a bike: it was a tandem, a very old one. My plan was to redo the trip, or at least part of it, but under far more enjoyable circumstances.

This book compares my memories of the trip I completed with my pal Alan back in the seventies, only a few years after Britain joined the EU, and the various parts of that trip, along with a few deviations, more than a few as it turned out, which I revisited just after Britain (or more correctly slightly more than fifty per cent of it) had voted to leave the EU. I certainly hope that full separation from Europe doesn't take place before the trip is over, or indeed ever, but that's a subject for a different book.

1976

USED CARS

I'd moved back to London after a brief spell in Manchester where I had ended up when a friend and I had decided we needed to leave the stultifying surroundings of our small town in Kent. Everyone from our area with any ambition of a more exciting life went to London so, just to be different we made the, in retrospect, for me at least, unwise decision to head further from home and settle in Manchester. There I'd lived in the suburb of Eccles for a while in a six-pounds-a-week, depressing bedsit with my old school friend John. Fairly soon after our arrival and, despite his close resemblance to a frog, John managed to find a girlfriend and spent most of his time with her, leaving me dejected and alone in our sad little room. I survived for a few months listening to the radio, writing long letters and bad poetry, but one chill December morn I'd had enough. I packed my few belongings and took a bus to Victoria bus station in London (the train was too expensive). There I hooked up with another friend from my schooldays, Ray. He was working in central London and shared a house with a group of schoolteacher acquaintances in an outer suburb of the sprawling capital. The house was already pretty full but they found room for me in a corner of one of the bedrooms. I laid out my sleeping bag, hung my few clothes in an already overfull wardrobe and called it home for a while. My presence decreased their rent and everybody, except the landlord, seemed happy with the arrangement. For a while at least.

I found a job in a car dealership in north London. Stoke Newington at the time was an interesting cultural melting pot. It consisted mainly of people who followed the Jewish faith and many descendants of immigrants from the Caribbean. This mix did not meet with my white supremacist boss' approval at all. The blatantly racist manager, who hailed from South Africa, took a shine to me for some reason. It may have been something to do with my borrowed suit, the trousers of which finished a good three inches above my shoes. In fact there were plans for me to accompany him on a tour of the North West. A return to the scene of the crime or as Henry would have put it, *the street of early sorrows*. None of this happened, as I only lasted three weeks in the job. No-one had told me I would have to work long hours including weekends and that I would only earn any real money if I actually sold a car. The short period I spent in London's multi-cultural northern suburb proved that selling anything was not my forté.

THE EAST ENDER

Apart from the unlikely existence of a burning desire to ride an ancient tandem across Europe with a stranger, one of the many reasons I embarked on my adventure was the fact that I did not feel, as has happened many times in my life, that my present employment was really what I wanted to do for the rest of my life, or indeed even close. Sometimes I did not even want to do it for the rest of the day.

Before signing up with Alan as second pedaller and assistant navigator on his exploration of Europe, I had spent six months employed by a 'finance' company which had its office in Oxford Street. One of the reasons I took the job was the location of the office, very close to the renowned and still extant 100 Club, the music venue where many famous bands had appeared even though it was only slightly bigger than most of its patrons' bed-sits. The Rolling Stones did a gig or two there when they were well into their fame and it's said that if you were there, you're lying. I had visions of bumping into Mick or Keef, fresh from rehearsal, as I left for home after another dull day of pen pushing and phone dialling. Needless to say it never happened.

Full details of how I had ended up as a trainee manager for what was, despite its lofty title, nothing more than a loan company, would not make interesting reading. Despite my scraggly beard and still being under the company's minimum employment age of twenty-one, a ruling doubtless laid down by some lackey in Human Resources (more accurately called Personnel in those days) to be considered for the job, after a short interview I was hired. The office manager was a gentle soul. Somehow, he saw past my badly matched, ill-fitting jacket and trousers, my never-fashionable yellow knitted tie, to the caring, conscientious, mature-beyond-my-years spirit that lay beneath.

I shaved off the beard and bought a new tie. Graham, my new boss and mentor, signed some sort of indemnity for the pen pushers in HR. And I was in. Glamorous as it may sound the job wasn't quite as impressive as I had led my parents to believe. I spent most of my time dialling the last known phone numbers of debtors. Having invariably failed to make contact with the penurious ones − *He's out. He's moved out and left the kids here; why don't you take them? Died.* − I would place a tick in the relevant box and move on to some other struggling soul. The most exciting period of my traineeship was the three months I spent on the road. 'On the Road' conjures up images of exciting adventures like those of Sven Hedin or Livingstone and, my namesake, Henry Morton Stanley.

Not exactly. I was not the first European to enter Tibet. Nor did I discover the source of the Nile, but I did once, almost inadvertently, successfully navigate the Hanger Lane gyratory system. On another occasion I circumnavigated London via both the North and South Circular roads in a single diurnal course. A record I like to think I hold to this day. The Royal Geographical Society never called.

In reality however, this was no Jack Kerouac-inspired, discovering the inner seeker type experience. No Neal, Dean or Sal to relate to and banter with at day's end for me.

It was hot, potentially dangerous and ultimately boring. I did get to listen to some great music on the car radio though.

England experienced two consecutive long hot summers in the seventies, 75 and 76. I spent the second of these driving around London in a Cortina Mark 3. As any *Top Gear* enthusiast will tell you this was the worst model. There was a reason Ford quickly rolled the Mark 4 off the production line.

Mostly my job consisted of attempting to physically locate, and, more importantly, extract money from, the same people who had refused to take my calls a couple of months earlier. Some, if not most of these characters were just sad individuals, not dissimilar to myself in many ways, who had incautiously borrowed money in an attempt to improve their mundane lives.

Stretched beyond their means, or made redundant, they had resorted to a quick cash fix for solace. A new TV or freezer, maybe nothing more exotic than buying their kids new bikes.

Others, and it was a small minority, were one step down from hardened criminals. Some days, as I sweated in the Cortina's vinyl seat and headed into the East End of London, I could almost smell the fear. Either that or I needed a better deodorant.

LONG HOT SUMMER

I should explain how I first met Alan, moreover how I ended up riding with him on our ill-fated trip. As I said, 76 had been a long hot summer and, perhaps perversely I wanted it to continue. Despite the life-threatening East End visits and clashes with acquaintances of the Krays I had enjoyed cruising the London streets in my Mark 3, windows down, stopping at friendly local stores for thirst quenching beverages and ice-cream. So when I saw an ad in *Time-Out* 'Seat available on tandem to warmer clime' I decided to investigate further.

I contacted the advertiser and we arranged to meet one balmy evening at Liverpool Street station. I suppose I was expecting some outward bound type: all blond hair and taut muscles with a healthy tan; he'd probably arrive in some crazy way, by helicopter perhaps or abseiling down the side of a building. So the wiry little guy with spectacles and an overly jutting chin who alighted from the 17:48 from Southend via Enfield that fateful Thursday evening came as something of a shock. We manfully shook hands and repaired to the station bar. Over pints of foaming ale plans were discussed. 'Plans' sounds much grander than the reality. This was no compass-based, poring-over-maps, take-the-wind-direction-and-elevation-into-account type conversation. 'I figure we cross The Channel and, basically, head south,' said Alan in his Essex accent. Who was I to argue with such faultless logic? So that's pretty much what we did.

DOWN TO KENT

After a few practice runs around the streets of Alan's neighbourhood we were ready to go. Alan turned out to be ahead of his time as a marketing guru and had arranged for the local paper, *The Enfield Gazette*, to interview us and take some pictures of us in our finery.

The first day of riding, which of course we didn't realize at the time, was one of the longest days of the whole trip. We rode from Alan's mother's house in Enfield, North London, to my parents' place in Herne Bay, Kent. Propelled by the enthusiasm of the new and with the bike in tip-top condition, relatively speaking, we whizzed along. Nearly a hundred miles in one day, we'd be in Athens in no time.

Route planning was never very detailed. One of the many O levels I had failed a few years previously, during my futile years at the Geoffrey Chaucer, was geography. But even I knew that travelling between Enfield and anywhere in Kent involved crossing the River Thames. The Dartford Bridge or Crossing, as it is officially known, had yet to be built and in 1976 the Dartford Tunnel was the only practical option. We couldn't just ride through the tunnel, much to our disappointment. We had to pay the princely sum of sixpence to have the beast put on a trailer and towed through. Alan had some hare-brained scheme of us both sitting in style on the tandem, wind blowing through our hair, as it was towed, with no little ceremony, perhaps some kind of fanfare playing through the vehicle's radio, as we raced through the tunnel. But of course, this was not allowed. Even in 1976 when smoking was still common, seatbelts were an option and we'd never heard of skimmed milk, there was still some concept of safety. So we sat in style in the van, with attached trailer, onto which was strapped our shiny two-wheeled, three-geared machine. Looking back it was probably my favourite part of the whole trip. Certainly it was the most comfortable.

Once through the tunnel we pedalled on via the historic Medway towns. I'd travelled many times between my Kent coastal hometown and the grand metropolis of London but always either by train or, if by car, using the M2 motorway. So it was quite a novelty to pass through towns like Rochester, Chatham and Sittingbourne instead of just seeing their names on station platforms or road signs. My impressions of these towns were that passing through them was the best thing to do.

WHAT'S A HOVERCRAFT?

There are many technologies which have come and, if not completely gone, their use has declined almost to the point of non-existence. These include such marvels as cassette tapes, public phone boxes and pocket calculators. The hovercraft should surely be included in this list. They do exist still but these days are mainly used for military purposes; their convenience as an option for public transport seems to have all but disappeared. There is a service from Southsea, in Hampshire, to Ryde, on the Isle of Wight but that is about the only one still operating, in Europe at least.

As a young traveller who lived in Kent, a stone's throw from 'the Continent' as many people erroneously called mainland Europe back then, the quicker I could get across The Channel the better. Nowadays of course there's a tunnel, much to many people's chagrin. But back in 76 it was a choice of at least a couple of hours on a frequently rolling, pitching ferry, which would in all likelihood reek slightly of chips, vomit and disinfectant, or that invention from the future, the hovercraft. Thirty minutes or so to almost fly across The Channel, in a vehicle from a sci-fi movie. The company which operated the services was even called Hoverspeed. Keen to embrace the future, and because it was cheaper than the ferry, we took the hovercraft across The Channel.

HONEYMOON NIGHT

I vividly remember our first night under canvas. Feeling pleased with ourselves for successfully navigating our way through the wilds of north-east Kent, surviving The Channel crossing and not being plunged in to the murky depths by the scudding hovercraft, we decided to break camp early at the first campsite we found just south of Calais. The sky was darkening and rain was forecast. Better to make sure we had a dry start to the trip. As we erected the tent Alan had the bright idea of using the fly sheet to protect the bike. If only I had realized then that his unwarranted desire to keep his beloved velocipede happy would override any logical thought, I would probably have walked back to Calais and taken the next England-bound transportation. I might even have considered swimming.

As expected it rained heavily. At some stage early in that long night I realized that, also as expected, without the protective second layer, the tent was flooding. This might have happened anyway eventually as rain was falling at quite a rate. But no doubt the inundation was exacerbated by not using the fly sheet on our aged tent for its intended purpose. I slept fitfully, drifting into short but deep periods of somnolence during which I would dream of refreshing slumber in a dry bed with a soft, feather-filled mattress and downy pillows, a gentle warm breeze from the open window caressing my face. The reality was the antithesis of my dream. Arms temporarily paralysed by lying on them to increase the space between my torso and the concrete-hard ground, the cold rough nylon of my cheap sleeping bag slipping and sliding in a surely possessed attempt to provide as little cover as possible. All this combined with the howling gale which had swept in, carried by Odin's Valkyries, from some uncharted part of Valhalla.

As the seemingly non-ending hours of darkness progressed I writhed in more and more discomfort, greater expanses of my bedevilled sleeping bag, and then my own aching body becoming sodden. Alan continued to snore peacefully beside me, manifestly unaware of the deluge outside or the increasing dampness within.

As the first pale light of the long-awaited dawn finally arrived we crawled ignominiously from our watery sleeping shelter. Alan was annoyingly pleased that the bike itself was hardly wet at all. His lack of concern that everything else had taken on more water than the Titanic irked me intensely. Not wishing to cause a scene so early in our relationship I remained stoic. We packed our wet belongings in silence, apart from Alan's tuneless, non-aspirated whistling, and readied our bedraggled bodies for departure. Silently we rode away from the quagmire where we had spent the night. It had stopped raining.

TOILETS AND HENRY

Because of our self-imposed budget restrictions, and in an effort to minimise weight, our toilet paper supplies were minimal. However due to the vagaries of our diet our lavatorial needs were not. Also, to avoid excess portage, reading materials were greatly limited.

I remember one occasion when we combined these two limitations by trying to share the reading of the one book Alan had packed, Henry Miller's *Plexus*. After a night or two of both of us trying to read it simultaneously, which did not work at all, not so much due to Alan's reading style being only slightly superior to that of a six-year-old, but more to the fact that the two of us snuggled together in our cheap, nylon sleeping bags conjured up, in my Henry Miller activated mind, a far too vivid, homo-erotic fantasy. This did not bode well for sleep or indeed the rest of the trip.

So we devised a strategy. Alan would read a few pages first, well it was his book, and then rip them from the spine for me to read. Alan's sloth-like reading pace resulted in me being able to properly digest the various tangents that constituted the bulk of Henry's superb writing. Plus it gave me the chance to doze off from time to time while Alan curled his tongue up to his top lip and attempted to read the more complex lines without resorting to actually enunciating them.

This evening reading ritual worked well and meant that the following morning we had a good supply of rather rough but perfectly usable toilet paper. We were sure that Henry wouldn't have minded us using his work in this manner. In fact we felt he would have applauded our resourcefulness. Was this not a man who, allegedly, had once cored an apple and used it for a not completely dissimilar purpose?

This inventive but perhaps not fully thought through strategy was probably responsible for blocking half the toilets in the campsites of France that year. *Plexus* is a big book.

SHOPPING FOR SPARES

We wandered the streets of Dijon searching unsuccessfully for a bike shop. One of the many problems with attempting to cross Europe on a British-made bike was the unavailability of parts. Europe of course uses the metric system and has done since 1799. England in 1976 did not. Some would say it still doesn't. Twenty-six inch tyres? ¾-inch bolt? Better planning would have meant us making at least some attempt to bring spare parts with us. But apart from 'head south' no such plans had been made.

Dijon is a beautiful city. It has a large number of churches, cathedrals and museums. It was also largely spared the destruction of wars and remains a jewel in France's cultural heritage. There's even a famous, if some-what nauseating, drink which originated there, named after the former mayor of Dijon canon *Félix Kir*.

We saw none of this and cared even less. We needed tyres and brake parts. It continued to rain heavily as we tramped the sodden streets and, as the late afternoon light faded into a misty darkness, I looked on enviously at well-dressed socialites enjoying steaming cups of hot chocolate as they chatted about their day's activities. Our search was fruitless and we returned to the campsite dejected and wet. Without the required spares the bike was simply unrideable. We crawled into the relative warmth of our tent, wondering what to do next. We realised that neither of us wanted to continue to endure the cold and damp conditions of October in Central France.

After much cajoling from me Alan reluctantly agreed that we should take the train south the following morning in an effort to find warmer, drier weather. I also successfully convinced him that there was bound to be a hidden English bike shop, probably very near to the station, when we arrived the next day in the more touristy part of the country. I slept well that night in the knowledge that, within a few short hours, I would be comfortably seated on a southbound train.

However the following morning the rain had stopped. Alan had been up ferreting about outside for a while, whistling tunelessly as ever, when I emerged from our plasticised dwelling. He looked entirely too pleased with himself. I knew he was about to say something I would not like. 'I fixed the bike', he chirpily announced. 'We can ride on'. I feigned what little degree of enthusiasm I could muster, 'Great, that's good'. I wept a little inside and steeled myself for more interminable days of discomfort.

ITALIAN LIFTS

The bike was not our only method of transportation. In the later stages of the trip I frequently wished it was not part of them at all. I would happily have taken a train. Frequently, general exhaustion, boredom, complete lack of any awareness of the direction to follow and various other reasons prompted us to find alternative methods of movement.

We even tried hitch hiking once or twice. Not easy with a hefty tandem, and our endeavour met with varying levels of success. Surprisingly it proved to be quite successful in Italy. Often we were picked up by amicable locals driving strange vehicles called *ape* or *bee*. These resembled the infamous Reliant Robin but were even less sturdy. Effectively a moped with a tin can attached to the back. Designed for the hard working, but financially struggling Italian artisan to carry tools, spare parts and of course a salami or two, they also provided space for a tandem and two English cyclists. The difficulty was that the lengthy tandem had to be held vertically. Bicycles are not designed to be transported in this fashion. Wheels have a propensity to want to revolve. This precarious form of transport saved us some time – and for me any time out of the saddle was welcome – but often, as we stood balanced precariously in the back of a friendly plumber's *ape*, valiantly ensuring the tandem didn't leap from the owner's vehicle and treading carefully among his pointed tools and dirty rags, we wondered if it wouldn't have been better to walk.

MORE TOILETS

One evening, after another long day of cycling we decided to treat ourselves to the luxury of an official campsite. The sky was transitioning through various shades of purple as we arrived at the *campeggio*. The campsite was located on an exposed bluff with late autumn winds howling in off the Adriatic. The *ufficio* was unmanned so we decided to save a few thousand lira by sleeping in the toilet block. The tent was barely offering any protection against the elements by this stage anyway and we had on a number of occasions considered offloading it. Alan seemed to have an unnatural connection to the orange nylon and was loath to just unceremoniously discard it.

The toilet block contained four separate shower cubicles but strangely no toilets. Luxury, single rooms. Except that we decided to relieve ourselves in two of them first. Naturally we did this in the two furthest from the door and the ever-strengthening storm outside. This left two in which to sleep. Cubicle one was adjacent to the gaping entrance and offered little protection from the wind, rain and, though they weren't yet visible, plagues of locusts that were doubtless about to descend from the tempestuous heavens. We steeled ourselves for another long night together and curled up in our sleeping bags on the concrete floor. At least we wouldn't need to go far for any calls of nature.

ROME, THE INFERNAL CITY

Rome is built on seven hills. I'm fairly sure we walked, rode and pushed our hefty bike up and down most of them. Yet again we were in search of spare parts. Here we were surrounded by more than 2000 years of culture and all we wanted was a new tyre. Needless to say, our search was fruitless. We found a couple of bike shops but once again the imperiousness of our transport could not be matched. I felt this was ironic as were we not after all in Imperial Rome? Should they therefore not have stocked the items we required in imperial sizes? Wrong empire.

The big city had one advantage over the numerous small towns we had been stopping in – food choices. Until now our diet had consisted mainly of whatever we could find, and afford, in bakeries and small shops along the route. But in the metropolis we salivated at the plethora of pizza, choice of cheese and mass of meat. As ever we could scarcely afford any of the delicacies on offer and, in retrospect, we were both happy to escape Rome's attractions and return to our peasant's diet of bread and cheese. Temptation is a terrible thing, especially when you can't afford it.

SOMEWHERE IN ITALY

I t may by now have become apparent that I have a liking for the writings of American author and bon vivant, Henry Miller. I'm no literary critic, all I know is that when I read his work I feel stirrings of passion in my own, often-cynical soul. So imagine my delight when on an otherwise uneventful coffee stop in rural Italy our paths crossed. Alan and I were struggling to make ourselves understood at the bar. This was mainly due to neither of us speaking more than the odd word of Italian. It had long ago become apparent that Alan had no language skills at all, at times he struggled to speak English, and even if I was proud to have recently learned the Italian for *open* and *closed,* none of my linguistic advances helped us to order any kind of refreshments. As I continued to try and construct a meaningful phrase out of my limited vocabulary *aperto, chiuso, cappuccino* and communicate with the frustrated bar owner, an elderly American entered the bar (I knew him to be American thanks to his headwear, a tattered baseball cap). Once he had helped us order our food and beverages we chatted for a while about how it was not hard to learn another language. I begged to differ and cited my monoglot cycling partner as a classic example. My new friend smiled irreverently and that's when I realised that he was none other than the salacious purveyor of literary porn, before such a thing even existed, Henry Miller himself.

Alan wasn't convinced: *I think he'd be a little more loquacious* was how he put it. A pretentious opinion if ever there was one. I remained certain and refused to be swayed from my conviction of our acquaintance's identity, even if I had to admit that Henry appeared somewhat shorter in real life than the few pictures I had seen of his wonderfully lived-in face. But there was no doubt in my mind, it was the New York-born Europhile himself.

We finished our drinks and left the bar to continue heading south. I pedalled along in a fame-induced daze wondering why such a literary giant was spending what must surely have been his last days in a small Italian provincial town. Should he not have been living in northern California with a buxom dark haired maiden? Such are the mysteries of life.

BRAKING (SIC) POINT

L ack of maintenance combined with a difficulty in obtaining spare parts gave rise to a number of interesting experiences.

Towards the end of our trip, somewhere in northern Greece we were descending a long hill. Our speed continued to increase and, as the designated front rider, I decided it was time to apply the brake. Yes I'm aware there should be two braking systems, one for the rear wheel and one for the front. I already knew the rear brake had long since ceased to function. Up to this point, until we could find replacement brake blocks, we had been managing with a single device. This dependency was about to come to an end.

As I cautiously squeezed the brake lever there was an ominous loud pinging sound. Wear and tear had caused a large discrepancy between the thickness of the blocks and, by simply obeying the immutable laws of physics, one had decided it would rather fly off and spend the rest of its rubbery life at the side of road somewhere in Greece. I had little time to dwell on the selfishness of this decision as I realized that without its colleague the lone block was unable to function. The laws of physics have no sympathy for lonely brake blocks however. Gravity continued to exert its undeniable force on the combined weight of our hefty bike, two cyclists whose subsistence diet of bread, pizza and cheese had long since taken its toll, combined with the various items of camping gear we were carrying, added a not insubstantial weight.

I knew what I had to do. Leaning forward I manually applied pressure to the remaining brake block so that it connected with the wheel rim. A risky manoeuvre as, if my finger slipped, it would simply be snapped off by the ever faster spinning spokes. I persevered, I really had no choice, and after five long seconds felt the beast beginning to lose momentum. As we slowed however, steering in my crouched position became more of a challenge. So now I was not only at risk of losing a digit or two but also of falling completely off the bike and being crushed by various haphazardly packed bags, a bespectacled companion and a far-from-lightweight tandem.

GREEK NIGHT

On arrival in Athens we decided it would be fun to sleep in the Acropolis. Not exactly in the buildings themselves, of which there are many, but in the gardens which surround them. The ground was surprisingly rocky, old stones and bits of plasterwork everywhere. The place really needed a good tidy up. We finally found an area of relatively smooth ground which, despite it being a bit gravelly, was perfectly adequate and certainly the equal of many of the other places we had spent the night. It was a mild evening so we didn't bother pitching the tent. Alan found a nice smooth area for the bike first of course and then we rolled out our sleeping bags as close to it as we could and settled down for the night. It was already dark anyway and the idea of a night under the stars appealed.

We slept well enough but were awoken early the following morning by streams of locals, giving us curious glances as they marched past on their morning commute. Only then did we realize that we had made camp on a footpath. This explained why it was so smooth.

HOMEWARD BOUND

Uncomfortable and monotonous as the cycling trip had not infrequently been, it simply did not compare to the utter drabness and deprivation of our return trip. The bike had long since given up the ghost. Only one of an already limited three gears remained, no brakes, and tyres that were held together by the thinnest of gossamer-like threads.

Our limited funds were almost depleted and on top of all of the other reasons not to even consider pedalling our way back to the isle of our respective births, it was late October. Spring may be considered glorious, a time of rebirth, when nature regains her loveliness. Autumn, certainly in Europe, is renowned for its dismal, wet and windy weather. Piles of russet leaves may be good subjects for the artist's canvas but they do not make for pleasant cycling. So, we caught the bus. This didn't seem like such a bad option. Yes it meant three days cramped in a 52 seater with no toilet. But at least we'd be rid of the bike. It had, in the latter days of the trip, become my nemesis and I had begun to view it as an albatross of travel. Many times I longed to awaken and find it damaged beyond repair by a nocturnal visitor or even better stolen by some misguided *vélovoleur*. 'Ah the little-known 1969, heavy-duty, hard-saddled, mid-framed tandem. I must have him.'

No such luck. Despite my frequent fantasies of last minute leaps as the rusting Raleigh plunged to its doom over a particularly precipitous cliff, Alan wanted to take it home! I was not so emotionally attached. I think he harboured dreams of repairing it and setting off on some other hare-brained adventure in the hills of Scotland or some such.

We had signed up to travel back to the UK on a bus operated by a company based in Newcastle. There were two drivers. Character wise they were polar opposites. D1 seemed amiable enough. A medium sized fellow with a kind face and a mop of unruly dark hair, through which he often ran his gnarled fingers. His co-driver descended from a different ape altogether, and judging by his demeanour, it had not been so long ago. Oafish in the extreme, with a sprouting mass of gingery grey hair, he exuded an air of barely concealed contempt for his charges.

The one thing they had in common was an impenetrable Geordie accent. That and a total aversion to ever stopping the lumbering monster they ruled over with absolute impunity. It was not uncommon to see a dishevelled passenger who, due perhaps to some unfortunate bladder condition required more than the arbitrary 60 second stop, running after the bus, one hand waving to attract attention while the other covered his still exposed manhood. I never saw any of the female passengers urinate as there simply wasn't time. I can only assume they held it for three days.

But the main thing I remember about the return trip was being permanently hungry. Our two drivers would only stop at certain food outlets, presumably those where they received a free meal from the owners for bringing in a large group of voracious travellers. Alan and I were among that number but we lacked the monetary wherewithal to sate our craving for sustenance. Instead we would roam the eatery of choice waiting for a dim-witted truck driver, gorged before his plate was clean, to leave and then, before a waiter could clear the table, pounce, wolf like, on any remaining food or beverage. Hygiene or the risk of contagion by an unwashed trucker's hand didn't enter our heads.

On arrival in Dover docks Rusty, as we had christened him, not so much because of his Celtic locks but more due to our supposition that his unwashed testicles were by now not dissimilar to the condition of the tandem's wheel rims, announced, in his strange vernacular, 'I've 'ad enough of this f**king bike' and looked as if he was about to hurl it into the foaming waves beneath the rocking boat. Alan was incensed and galvanised into action. He rushed forward – I was reminded of an angry dog readying itself to attack his master's assailant – and heroically grasped the bike. He gently and with, I felt, an unnecessary degree of reverence laid it down on the glistening tarmac. Turning our backs on our fellow travellers we mounted and without further ado rode, somewhat waveringly, across the windswept car park. Once away from the floodlights' glow we stopped and gingerly returned to pick up our minimal but still important luggage. Rusty glared at us as if we had molested his sister (something, we felt, he would have probably have rather done himself). 'Go on, f**k off yer buggers' were the last words we heard from his simian mouth.

What the self-styled Grand Master of the Omnibus didn't know was that, due to a state of advanced pecuniary inadequacy, before our Hellenic departure we had done a deal with the similarly desperate Athens travel agent to pay the remainder of our twenty-five pounds fare on arrival. In fact so keen was he to sell two more seats on the end-of-season northbound transport that he had agreed to only five pounds each as a deposit. 'The rest you can pay in Newcastle,' he had foolishly uttered. F**k you Rusty.

HOME FOR A WHILE

The ride and homeward journey complete I returned to my dull, unfulfilling life in Herne Bay, disappointed that the bike trip had not, as I had naively thought it would, drastically changed or improved my life. I stumbled in to another tedious job, this time in Canterbury, the nearest large town. Personal relationships developed and faded. My days passed slowly until an opportunity came around for me to move to Germany and work for a local council there. I quit my latest depressing job without further ado and made arrangements to travel to Germany.

A BIT ABOUT HERNE BAY

My parents moved to Herne Bay in Kent from the south London suburb of Crystal Palace when I was seven years old. I like to say I caught up with them a year or so later, but of course the family all moved at the same time. For reasons unknown to me the move took place on 1 January 1963. Europe and therefore England experienced one of its worst-ever winters that year, so exactly why we moved right in the middle of it I cannot imagine. For contractual reasons I assume. While it must have been a nightmare of organization for my parents, for me it was all a grand adventure. I remember taking a bus from Crystal Palace – the family didn't own a car – and then a train from Victoria Station to Herne Bay. Quite how we got from the station to the dilapidated house my father had purchased for him and my mother to run as a guest house, I don't recall. I can't believe we walked as it was a few miles from the station and can only assume we must have taken a taxi. Such extravagance. We may have been collected but as we knew no-one in town that seems unlikely. The pantechnicon carrying our furniture, and my toys, got stuck in snowdrifts and so we arrived to an empty, freezing, possibly haunted house. Some old furniture, left by the previous owners and destined for destruction, was set up as temporary accommodation and we settled down for the night. I remember my father sleeping on a wooden upright chair; he told me later he could sleep anywhere and had often dozed off, standing up, on the tube in London. Needless to say I believed him, seven-year-olds believe everything and assume their father is a font of all knowledge. The pantechnicon finally arrived at three in the morning and the removal guys were accommodated in freezing beds until the morning.

Life as a kid wasn't so bad in Herne Bay. I walked to school and made new friends. We lived at the seaside, what could be better? As I later found out, living somewhere with a warmer climate for a start. But, knowing no better, I learned to swim in the chill, grey-green waters of the North Sea and happily rode my bike everywhere in all weathers, something I could never have done had we stayed in London. When I grew up I lamented my parents' decision to move out of the city. Surely had we stayed there, I would have witnessed the excitement of the swinging sixties and loon-mad seventies first hand. I would have been able to go to concerts and see all my musical heroes live. I would have wandered into some long demolished pub and witnessed Fleetwood Mac, with Christine McVie and Jeremy Spencer of course. Or even better Chicken Shack with the glorious Christine Perfect as she was known then, singing the blues. Who knows how different my life might have been. Herne Bay seemed caught in a fifties' time warp in comparison. Certainly there wasn't much of a music scene there. The more adventurous and wealthy resident could go to Canterbury where a number of well-known bands often played at the university. The pub music scene didn't really exist at that time so for the most part, as a budding music lover, I was restricted to the radio, or playing to death the odd album or single purchased, or surreptitiously filched, from the local music store. There was small, rather sad looking youth club in town, which I would frequent on a Friday night, when some long-haired DJ (in fact a geography teacher from the local school) would play the latest hits while we shuffled around and tried to pluck up the courage to ask the girls to dance. One evening one of the local hooligans decided he didn't like my answer of 'actually I don't really like football' to his inane 'what football team do you support?' question and tried to pick a fight. I decided it was time for more esoteric pursuits.

For all of us there are certain pivotal moments in time. Specific actions or coincidences that push us in a certain way and mould us for the remainder of our lives, where we remain until the next swirling eddy takes us, unyielding, down a different tributary and into a different stream.

It seemed that, during my formative years, wherever I went in the world on my adventures I was always drawn back to Herne Bay. It was for more than twenty years the inescapable black hole of my life's journey.

Then there was my working life. As a teenager – living it seemed only a few years after child labour was banned in England – I did the standard early morning paper rounds for a pittance. How well I remember the winters struggling along the exposed sea front with my heavy bag weighed down by newspapers to be delivered. After a year or two I graduated from paper rounds and once earned the princely sum of fifty pence a week doing a butcher's round. The butcher's round was a definite step up the ladder for two reasons; it was only one day a week, and I got to use one of those special delivery bikes with a small front wheel to accommodate a huge basket on the front. The basket was full of choice cuts of meat and, nearing Christmas, giant turkeys. Controlling this front-heavy monstrosity was quite a challenge. Such bikes are seldom seen these days.

By far my most interesting schoolboy job was that of a bingo arcade attendant. So enamoured was I with this introduction to the world of entertainment that, even once I had left school and started my real career with its daily commute to London, I carried on working in the arcade for a couple of summers. This supplemented the paltry sum I was paid, on a monthly basis, by the insurance company I worked for in London. Often, when I had enjoyed a lifestyle beyond my means and spent my salary well before the end of the month, the few extra pounds I earned at the arcade kept me alive, or at least supplied with beer and cigarettes.

The Pier Arcade was managed by the owner's son, a friendly, crew-cut-sporting guy, called Bill. I started out charged with the simple task of supplying change to the patrons, but once Bill realized I was slightly more intelligent that his other employees I graduated to the heady realm of caller, a task Bill usually kept for himself. The arcade was one of the few family-run entertainment businesses in town. Most of the other amusement arcades were franchises of some kind and the other main bingo arcade was a swanky place a little further along the sea front called, rather ostentatiously, The Connaught Lounge. I never went in there as the minimum entry age was twenty-one. I could only imagine how decrepit the patrons must be, but it also purported to be a dance hall, whatever that might be. I could not imagine ever being so old, or indeed, ever wanting to dance in the way those old people did.

THE YEARS IN BETWEEN

GERMANY

I t's hard now to imagine how difficult it was in those pre-internet days to plan even a simple journey over-seas. Apart from visiting a travel agency there was no effective way to compare prices and options for travel. Most travel agencies were only interested in offering package tours of some kind and could offer little help to an independent traveller like me. I made my own arrange-ments knowing that another ferry trip and train or bus across Europe was my only limited choice.

The ferry crossing from Dover was rough and I arrived in Zeebrugge minus the contents of my stomach. A fresh start in more ways than one I thought. I boarded a train to Dortmund excited by the fact that this same train went all the way to Moscow via Berlin and Warsaw. Journeys for another time. I shared the compartment with another young traveller heading for Berlin to take up some kind of internship. He spoke German well and gave a glowing account of what I could expect in his adopted country. I'd just finished reading Henry's only travel book *The Colossus of Maroussi*, a colourful account of my hero's stay in pre-

Second World War Greece, and I gave this to my new friend to accompany him on his remaining long train journey.

In Germany I was lodging with a window who had, to me, an almost unpronounceable surname. I promised myself that once I could pronounce it I would be officially integrated into life in Germany. But I had some other hurdles to cross first. One of these was the German work ethic. My first job was on a building site where an enterprising fellow was building a theme park. The job wasn't glamorous in any way, I was just a labourer on a building site, but I still felt more fulfilled than I had in a long while. My lack of practical skills, and complete ignorance of the German language, meant that I was only considered fit for the most mundane of tasks – digging ditches or cleaning equipment after the more qualified members of the group had used them. I developed blisters in places where I didn't know I had places.

It wasn't just hard labour though. I have some happy memories:

Beer for breakfast.

Learning passable German in six weeks. More than forty years later I still remember the first phrases I mastered, 'Sauber machen, clean it' invariably followed by 'Nicht sauber, not clean'.

Soon however, often aided by that breakfast beer, I was eloquently employing complicated grammatical structures and, as long as I didn't say too much, was even from time to time mistaken for a local. It is possible that may have been due to the luxuriant beard I had cultivated along with an ever burgeoning stomach. Beer again. I could by now easily pronounce my landlady's name, *Niestadtkoetter*.

My apparent linguistic ability proved to me that immersion is the best way to learn anything. I consequently lived for ten years in France and although my French is passable I still feel more confident speaking German. Having learnt the language, in situ, I also know many words that should not be used in polite company. And some very politically incorrect jokes. Buy me a beer and I'll tell you one.

OVERLAND TO INDIA

My year in Germany had taught me a few things, among them the fact that physical labour was not for me. It had also allowed me to save a fair bit of money which I wanted to spend fulfilling a lifelong dream to visit India. I didn't expect to attain any kind of enlightenment, in fact I have no idea why I became so obsessed with travelling there. It was just something I wanted to do. I devoured as many books as I could on the journey I knew I would one day make myself. My procrastination almost scuppered any possibility of doing the trip at all as only weeks after I had travelled through Iran and Afghanistan both of these countries were thrown into total confusion by revolution and religious-based turmoil. Unaware of the complex politics of the countries I was going to pass through, I finally set off one cool September morning.

Many books have been written over the years covering the classic Overland to India route. This is not one of them. I only remember certain parts of the journey. First, the inevitable cross-channel ferry, a smooth crossing this time which I took as a good omen. I spent the night in Paris, sleeping in a tiny apartment owned by an acquaintance of a friend. He was an artist of some kind and used the apartment as a studio to work and store his artistic efforts. It wasn't really set up for guests but I slept well on the floor between strangely coloured canvases, brushes and paints.

The next morning found me at the Gare de l'Est boarding a train bound for Venice, Italy. The train travelled overnight – I planned most of the journey through Europe this way to avoid accommodation costs. Arriving in Venice by train is indeed spectacular. Alan and I had passed through Venice some years before with the tandem but were forced to stay some way away from the main town as tandems are not really welcome or practical on the canals. Also we were camping and Venetian infrastructure was not then, and is not now, geared up for campsites. I'm not sure what I expected when I alighted from the train and made my way outside but I was quite taken aback at the picture postcard beauty of it all. I wasn't staying in Venice though. For a few hours I wandered the streets, surprised that there actually are streets in Venice, before heading back to the station and catching another train bound for Belgrade in what was then still Yugoslavia.

In Belgrade I had the address of another friend of a friend who would hopefully put me up for a night or two. I also had directions to where he lived which went something like *take bus number 32 from the station to the cemetery.* Somehow I found my way to Sinisia's house but he wasn't home. He lived with his grandmother who spoke no English but, like many older Eastern Europeans, did speak some German. She welcomed me in, gave me something to eat and drink and we attempted polite conversation until Sinisia came home.

After a couple of interesting days in Belgrade with Sinisia as my guide I was back at the station again, this time for the final leg in Europe to Istanbul. On the long train journey into the unknown I befriended an American professor who had a connection to a university in Istanbul. I think this may have been due to his love of smoking which seemed to be the Turkish national sport. He lit one cigarette after the other as we chatted through the evening. To save money we ended up sharing a room in Istanbul and he continued to smoke incessantly there.

The following morning, after a couple of cigarettes, we parted company and I never saw him again.

I spent a pleasant couple of days exploring the delights of Istanbul before taking a bus to Erzurum in the east of the country. On the eve of my departure, concerned and uncertain how long the trip to the bus station, located in the outskirts of the city, would take, I made one of the many mistakes of travel. I told the taxi driver taking me there that I was in a hurry. He rose to the challenge by driving even more insanely than seemed to be the norm in Turkey. We careened through the crowded streets, over-taking everything in sight. Once I reached the bus station and located my bus I realized I still had at least an hour before its departure. There was no sign of the driver and everyone was happily eating kebabs, drinking tea, and smoking.

The bus rumbled out of town and we drove through the night into the unknown. My seat partner was very friendly and kept me supplied with a constant stream of Marlboros. At meal stops he insisted on ordering for me and paying. When I tried to give him a small amount which I thought would cover the costs of the food, he refused to accept it. Eventually we arrived in Erzurum and I found somewhere to stay. As I entered the reception area of the small hotel I had selected, I came across an English girl trying to converse with the owner in German. Her German was not very good and there was obviously some confusion about whatever it was they were trying to sort out. My linguistic genius came to the fore and I helpfully translated. It transpired she was organising a taxi for some kind of expedition the following day and the confusion stemmed from the pick-up time. In English we express the half hour as past the hour; in German it's the opposite so *halb acht* (half eight) is not half past eight, it's half to eight, or in English half past 7 or 7:30. Once arrangements had been confirmed she asked me if I would like to join her and her friends on a visit to some nearby caves the next day. I had no plans and gladly agreed. Victoria, Charles and Georgie were a strange trio. Hailing from one of the more upmarket London suburbs they too were heading for India. Charles had recently left the army while Victoria and Georgie (short for Georgina) had been 'working in fashion'. I could just imagine them in the local wine bar one evening, having a jolly good time, I'm sure, when apropos of nothing in particular Charles had suddenly announced, 'I'm going to travel overland to India, who's in?'

I stuck with the trio for a few days. Travelling alone has many advantages but it's also good to have some company from time to time. We crossed the border into Iran and stayed with acquaintances of the Sloane Rangers in Tehran. I began to find myself attracted to Georgie, which I knew could only end badly. Human emotions never make a lot of sense. She was as upper class, and frankly, annoying, as her buddies but as the days passed I found her little-girl-lost manner strangely alluring. This untenable situation came to a head in Tehran, where we were staying in an apartment near the Iraqi embassy. Relationships between the two countries in early 1979 were not good but full scale war had not yet broken out.

As wandering the streets of Tehran was not recommended, we spent a lot of time in the apartment with the official residents. During this time Georgie started an affair with one of the guys who lived there. I should have simply bidden everyone farewell and moved on immediately. But I was a little worried about travelling on alone and thought it best to remain with the famous three despite the difficult situation, purely of my own making, with Georgie. A week or two later, after some enthusiastic locals started throwing stones at a bus we were on, we left Tehran together heading ever eastwards towards the border with Afghanistan. In light of the possible dangers we might face we made a pact to continue travelling together through Afghanistan as far as Kabul. There were no long goodbyes in Kabul and we all happily went our separate ways pleased that an embarrassing situation had ended. In Kabul I met a guy called John who was headed my way. We travelled together for a while, crossing the Khyber pass into Pakistan and taking trains across the country and over the Indian border to Delhi via a stop in beautiful Amritsar.

My unsuccessful dalliance with Georgie did not dampen my mood for long and once I reached India it lightened even further. John and I travelled together for a few weeks and finally parted ways in Pune where he was planning to stay on a retreat for an extended period of time to study yoga. I continued my journey south enjoying a carefree couple of weeks taking trains to places that sounded interesting but were often not. My desire to avoid the hippies meant bypassing Goa which everyone seemed to visit. I did find myself on Kovalam beach one day, which back in 1979 was almost unknown, apart from by the laid-back hippies. These days there are five star hotels and beach resorts everywhere.

My Indian sub-continent experience continued for three more months with time in Nepal, where I trekked in the Himalayas, and Sri Lanka where I almost drowned. There were a number of other firsts. My first international flight was from Kathmandu, Nepal to Patna in India. This was a fairly common and financially rewarding way to exit the Himalayan Kingdom for backpackers like me. The other way out entailed a rugged three day road journey. Although the flight seemed expensive, the hidden advantage was that you could buy cigarettes and whisky in Kathmandu and sell them at a handsome profit in Patna as neighbouring Bihar State in India was officially a dry state where alcohol sales were banned.

Travelling the length of the country again by train and bus and crossing the strait between India and Sri Lanka, I arrived almost penniless on the tear-shaped island that hangs off the southern tip of India. I had taken the ferry from Rameswaram to Talaimannar, a service which used to run regularly. Sadly the long-running Sri Lankan civil war put an end to the ferry service and, despite numerous discussions and proposals, it is yet to be re-instated. Although I was now running low on funds I saw a fair bit of the country before taking my first ever inter-continental flight. Not many airlines flew to or from Sri Lanka in those days and the only one I could afford was the infamous Russian carrier Aeroflot. My flight left from Colombo, capital of Sri Lanka to London via Moscow with a refuelling stop in Tashkent. It all seemed so exciting and exotic.

LONDON AND THE TOURIST BOARD

I had returned from my six months on the Indian subcontinent with a mild case of hepatitis. As I convalesced at my parents' small bungalow on the edge of town I wondered what I would do next. Inevitably I ended up in London. This time the job I found myself in was not so bad. For once in my life my previous experience actually came in useful. As I said earlier, I had learned passable, if not fluent, German during my year or so living and working there. This, along with a vague memory of schoolboy French, helped me obtain a job offering assistance and tourist information to newly arrived visitors to London. The London Tourist Board, or LTB as it was known, had a small office, no more than a booth really, on Victoria Station and a larger office located nearby on Buckingham Palace Road. A group of us, all affable and multilingual – most of my colleagues were far more quali-fied for the job than I was – assisted confused newcomers to the capital with hotel bookings and other useful infor-mation. I still remember some of the more inane questions:

What time is the last bus? OK, and what time is the one after that?

Can you recommend a place where we can dance and eat at the same time?

Because part of the job involved booking hotel rooms for visitors, we were often invited for drinks and low-key cocktail parties at many of the local hotels in the inner London area. Still recovering from my bout of hepatitis I was unable to drink alcohol, or smoke, and this seemed to make me, for once in my life, strangely attractive to women. Sadly this new found attribute seldom led to any physical contact. I think the girls just thought I needed looking after and would often wonder why I had failed to iron my shirt or press my trousers. It could be that my temporary sobriety allowed me to be more aware of other people's feelings and therefore less obnoxious than usual. It didn't last. I'd been told by my doctor not to drink or smoke for six months and I was careful to heed his warning. Six months to the day I consumed a vast amount of red wine and returned to my normal status of *loser extraordinaire* with my few lady friends. I felt much happier with this arrangement.

6 MONTHS ON THE KIBBUTZ

As the short British summer drew to a close and with a few hundred pounds in my pocket I set off on my travels again. I decided to follow up on a vague notion of heading for Israel to try spending time on a kibbutz. A colleague at the LTB had a relative who lived on a kibbutz located just north of Tel Aviv, so with the address scribbled in my notebook I took a bus to Athens with no real plan as to how I would complete the journey to Israel. I'd done my share of long distance bus travel before and knew what to expect, but this particular journey was exceptionally awful. Before the advent of low cost air carriers the cheapest way to travel between London and Athens was always the bus. Trains were an option but still relatively expensive although doubtless far more comfortable. So I boarded a fairly new-looking bus along with various other cheapskates and we headed off. I remember very little about the journey and it was only when leafing through some old letters I had written to my parents that I noticed I had told them the journey had taken four days as opposed to the usual three. It seems, or so I wrote, this was due to bad weather in the Alps necessitating a detour via southern France. Obviously the journey must have been so tedious and uncomfortable that I have simply obliterated any memory of it.

From Athens I took a cheap flight to Tel Aviv. The address my ex-colleague had given me was in a suburb of Tel Aviv and I managed to somehow find my way there. The elderly lady I met there was pleased to see me and gave me the address of the kibbutz where her daughter worked. Communication was not easy. She spoke very little English and I spoke no Hebrew. Fortunately, like many older Israelis and Jews worldwide she spoke Yiddish. I spoke passable German and somehow through these distantly related languages we managed. I think she understood a lot more of what I said than I did of what she said. As I slowly began to pick up a few Hebrew words and phrases I became intrigued as to why the name *Ken* was mentioned so often. It took me a few days to realize that *Ken* is the Hebrew word for *Yes*. It's all gone now but I did learn the Hebrew alphabet and, even if I couldn't write anything meaningful, I would often amuse myself and attempt to impress people, or more accurately, girls by transliterating their name from English to Hebrew characters.

I boarded a bus and headed north with the address of the kibbutz written in both English and Hebrew on a scrap of paper. I was a bit concerned when, at one of the many stops en route, a group of heavily armed soldiers boarded the bus. But it turned out they were just passengers also heading north and once they had rested their semi-automatics in the luggage rack they sat down and started playing cards. We wove our way through the outskirts of Tel Aviv and after another couple of hours the driver slowed and shouted something in my direction. I failed to comprehend at first as he seemed to be saying something like *giboo chivat chaim chad*. I eventually understood. Hebrew is a wonderfully expressive and guttural language and my destination was *Kibbutz Givat Hayim Meuchad*. I alighted from the bus with my small bag expecting some kind of entrance, or at least a sign. The ever helpful if somewhat incomprehensible driver pointed down a deserted side road off to the left of the main highway, *Kibbutz, 3 kilometre* he said smiling.

The bus soon disappeared in a cloud of diesel fumes and I had no choice but to begin walking in the direction the driver had indicated. A certain calm descended as I strolled through the orange orchards which bordered the road. A few cars and trucks passed but otherwise it was very quiet and still. After a while I came across a small gate with the words *Kibbutz Givat Hayim Meuchad* written on it, fortunately for me in both English and Hebrew (I later learned that the *Meuchad* part was there because of a sister kibbutz on the other side of the road called *Givat Hayim Ihud*). Originally there had been one kibbutz but in 1952 ideological differences had caused a rift and one kibbutz had become two kibbutzim. There was no sign of any security which, especially after the soldiers on the bus, surprised me. Not wishing to arouse suspicion I walked quickly through the gate and onto the kibbutz.

The place seemed deserted but it later transpired that I had somehow entered via a side gate, reserved for those working in the fields, which had inadvertently been left open. I chanced upon a friendly kibbutznik who showed me the way to the office, and where the main entrance, security gate and car park were located. The staff were quite surprised that I had just turned up. Most volunteers were part of a larger group who had signed up for a specific period through an agency, most of which were located in the UK and Scandinavia.

I was allocated a billet in one of the barrack-like accommodation units. Very few volunteers had private accommodation so I shared with a slightly eccentric American fellow who distinctly resembled Radar from the TV show *M.A.S.H.* He called himself Brillo for reasons I never discovered, just as I never knew his real name. More for my own amusement than anyone else's I called our small plywood and cement living space Brillo's pad – an obscure reference to a cleaning product popular in Britain at that time.

During my tenure in Israel I did a number of jobs – washing dishes, milking cows, and the most common task on most kibbutzim, picking fruit – but the highlight was when I was selected to work in the turkey farm. My role was part of a team of inseminators. It's a little known fact that a male turkey produces enough sperm to fertilise approximately 125 females, so it would be bad management indeed to just let them please themselves. As the farm was in the business of selling fertilised eggs to other farms it was necessary to intervene in the natural process and ensure that as many females, or more correctly, their eggs, were fertilised as possible. The process was surprisingly simple. Three of us worked together as a unit. One person, usually the most experienced member of the team, would sit, regally, in a large specially designed chair. Next to the chair was a mobile fertilisation unit. Effectively a pump with a small nozzle attached. I'm going to leave it to the reader's imagination where that nozzle had to be inserted and what the pump did.

The turkeys, all female, had to be coaxed along a laneway from their respective sheds and strongly encouraged to step onto a short conveyer belt: the turkeys always seemed to enjoy this part. Getting the dumb birds onto the conveyer belt involved a third person. Their responsibility was to wave two large sticks with flags attached behind the turkeys so that, in their scared reaction to escape whatever it was that was behind them, invariably a sleepy and slightly bored volunteer, they would scurry in the direction of the belt.

Once the ride was over the second member of the team was charged with grabbing them by the legs, upending them and placing them between the legs of the inseminator. They would usually ride the conveyer belt quite happily but once grabbed by the legs, as would anyone, they began to fight back and flap their wings quite aggressively at the grabber and finally the inseminating machine.

This job did involve some very early mornings. The birds were less active and therefore easier to manage before dawn. Depending on the number to be inseminated, which varied from day to day, I would start work at three, four, or five am. In addition to that, for health reasons – the birds' not mine – I was expected to shower before starting work. Even in Israel it can be quite cold early in the morning so I soon devised a ploy to avoid the early morning shower. I realized after a few weeks that if I arrived at the sheds a minute or two before the rest of my team, I could circumvent the early morning ablutions by turning on the shower but not actually using it. When my colleagues arrived they would see the wet floor and assume I had obeyed instructions and was fully cleansed before going near their beloved turkeys.

To compensate for the pre-dawn starts there were a number of positive aspects to my new career. As the sheds were located a fair way from the main kibbutz I was given a bike so that I could ride to my place of work. I got to use the bike for personal trips as well so would often ride to the beach on my day off. Also, due to the early start and the distance I was from the main dining hall, I ate breakfast in a special room with the turkey team. An additional perk was that I also got to take home as many eggs, which for one reason or another had failed to be fertilised but were still perfectly fine for eating, as I liked. Not good for my cholesterol I'm sure, but a pleasant change from the normal kibbutz diet.

What I have not yet described, and what I'm sure readers are dying to know, is where we obtained the required semen to carry out the whole process. Sitting majestically in a special warm, well ventilated shed were a small number of male turkeys. Before entertaining the ladies we had to extract the required liquid from the males. Mostly this was a fully automated process in which I was never involved. I assumed it required far more training than was considered worth giving to a volunteer who would in all likelihood decide to leave the kibbutz at any time. However occasionally there would be a male who, while fully functional in all other respects, was being kept away from the other males, usually due to some minor turkey ailment such as a skin disorder which could quickly spread. Setting up the extraction paraphernalia for just one bird was not deemed worth the effort so his seed would be collected, literally, by a manual process. This involved touching the little feller in a certain part of his anatomy and using a pipette to collect the resulting issue. Needless to say it was not a popular task and I'm sure the regulars were happy to let it fall to a volunteer. I sometimes wondered if it wasn't all some elaborate Israeli joke.

COPENHAGEN

During my last weeks working with the turkeys on the kibbutz I'd befriended a charismatic guy called Michael. He was outrageously gay and came from Dublin. Before arriving on the kibbutz Michael had been living in Copenhagen and working in a large hotel. He offered to help me find a job at the hotel and to share his apartment in the Danish capital. We really had very little in common but for some reason became close friends. Only later did I discover that Michael was secretly in love with me and, mistakenly, assumed me to be of the same sexual persuasion as himself. Our co-habitation in his apartment in Copenhagen didn't last very long but the few months I spent in his company were interesting to say the least. Michael was a colourful character and in the time I knew him we had some memorable experiences. He took me to a few clubs where, due I suppose to my good looks and quiet nature, plus the fact that I was in a gay club with another man, people assumed I was gay. On many occasions I was having what I assumed to be a friendly chat with some well-dressed fellow when he would decide to stroke my beard or squeeze my leg. In my naivety I just assumed this was an overt display of friendliness but if, as they sometimes did, the overtures became more obvious I would just smile and say I had to leave.

The situation changed when I met a woman called C. Michael wasn't impressed. I think he knew fairly quickly after our move to Copenhagen that I wasn't interested in him as a sexual partner, but we still got on well, and, despite the polarity of our personalities, enjoyed each other's company. When C moved in to the apartment with me he decided he'd had enough and unceremoniously asked, or rather told, us to leave. C and I looked around for alternative lodging and eventually found a small room available in a house in another part of the city. We set up home there – as much as a mattress and a small table can be called home – and I continued working at the hotel. I naively thought our relationship was blossoming and imagined it lasting forever. But I was mistaken and when I returned home one evening C simply said, *This isn't working out. I'm moving back to Dublin*. I, of course, was devastated.

RETURN TO INDIA AND AUSTRALIA
TRIP ONE

After the break up I felt the need to escape. We tell ourselves that travel will help us forget someone. It doesn't of course. Usually the often-extreme loneliness of travel simply exacerbates the intensity of romantic feeling and the pain becomes worse. In my case I set off for India and Australia on a misguided trip with someone who turned out to be a completely unsuitable travelling partner. I'd known Derek for a while; we worked together in the hotel in Copenhagen. He seemed amiable enough on first meeting and we got on well at work as we devised ways to avoid spending any more time than absolutely necessary to complete any of the menial tasks allotted to us. We'd socialised a little and it was when Derek had a drink inside him that his mood changed. He hailed from Leith, an apparently beautiful coastal suburb of Edinburgh, Scotland. Derek was intensely proud of his heritage and took particular exception to ever being mistaken for an Englishman. This is understandable, certainly justifiable in many circumstances, but when visiting India, where the locals might from time to time fail to distinguish between the various tribes that make up Great Britain, it only led to confusion and unnecessary arguments.

Derek's unforgiving nature often showed itself in bizarre ways. One evening, relaxing in one of Copenhagen's many excellent drinking establishments he had taken umbrage at some innocent comment and, turning his chair round to face away from his cohorts he aggressively stated, *I can't look at you fools anymore.* Funny for a while but Derek obstinately stayed in this position all evening. It made further conversation a challenge.

Because I wanted to be as far away as possible from the source of my broken heart, and even knowing Derek's bad side, I decided travelling to Australia with him would be OK. We found a cheap flight to Sydney on Air India. This suited me perfectly as it allowed an overland stretch from Bombay up to Delhi. Having visited India a few years previously I had long wanted to re-visit and explore in a bit more depth. India affects people in different ways. It seemed to agree with Derek and, apart from the odd argument about why Scotland should not be considered part of the UK and certainly was not the same as England, the few weeks we spent there went well.

Ultimately I had to admit that Derek was not the best of travelling companions. With the benefit of hindsight I'm convinced that, despite my desperation to be reunited with C, had it not been for Derek's unpredictable character, I would have stayed on in Sydney longer and not made the disastrous decision to leave Australia just before Christmas and go to Dublin on what can only be described as a fool's errand.

DISASTER IN DUBLIN

Having successfully persuaded the Air India staff in Sydney that I simply had to be home for Christmas due to a family emergency, I spent a day or more on various planes and arrived back in Europe a few days before Christmas Day. Unfortunately I was on the right continent but I was in the wrong country. When Derek and I had booked our flights we had been living in Copenhagen. Air India didn't fly to Sydney from Copenhagen but they did from the relatively close German city of Frankfurt. We'd taken a bus from Copenhagen down through southern Denmark and northern Germany to fly out. Logically my many connecting flights terminated in Frankfurt as well. I was stranded there a few days before one of the busiest days of the year. My desire to be reunited with C outweighed any logical thought so I purchased a one-way ticket, in business class – all that was available –between Frankfurt and Dublin via London. Looking back, it was the beginning of the end. My savings were already being seriously depleted. None of this mattered when I arrived victorious at Dublin airport and C was there to meet me. But it all went rapidly downhill with alarming speed.

The Dublin situation didn't work out for many reasons. Perhaps I expected too much. Doubtless I was obsessed and blinded by love. C was back among friends she had before she met me and, while I think she tried to help me fit in and become part of her old life, I simply wasn't able to. We struggled along for a few months. I found some lodgings and a job in town. In 1981–82 Dublin had one of the worst winters of the century. It was bitterly cold and snowed heavily, unusual for Ireland which lies in the Gulf Stream and generally had mild, if wet, winters. There were many snow related stories going around the pubs, including one that the Dublin council had one snow plough but it was stuck in the snow.

I'd arrived in December of 1981, straight from a Sydney summer. Trudging the streets in my cheap plastic shoes, I frequently wondered if I had made the right decision. I worked for a few nights in the kitchens of a well-known hotel. Much as I tried to convince myself this was useful experience and that like George Orwell slaving as a *plongeur* in Paris, I would soon be writing my first book, I hated every minute of it. I eventually obtained more gainful employment at a major retailer and began to cultivate my own small circle of friends. But C didn't seem interested in putting in the effort required to maintain our relationship and it faltered even further. So one early spring morning as the winter, in a final display of irony, seemed to be finally releasing its grip on the Emerald Isle, I headed for Dún Laoghaire, took the ferry to Holyhead and a bus to London. It was all over.

Many years later when I returned to Dublin on a business trip, I could not help but be secretly disappointed to notice, as the taxi taking me to the airport, by a strange twist of fate, drove passed the single room where I used to live, that there was no blue plaque on the wall celebrating my joyless, love-wrenched residence there.

THE LONDON DEPRESSION

S amuel Johnson famously said that *when a man is tired of London, he is tired of life*. This adage definitely applied to me. On my return to London I'd failed to be re-employed by the LTB and had a string of uninspiring travel related jobs in equally uninspiring offices scattered around the city. I spent most of my spare time attempting unsuccessfully to persuade C to join me in London. She failed to relent apart from one unexpected visit which left me feeling even more confused and wretched than ever.

My string of futile employment in badly paid jobs continued until one day I spotted an advert for trainee instructors with a well-known driving school. Three items caught my attention: *Training included. Unlimited earnings. Freedom*. The reality turned out to be somewhat different. Training was included but the cost of it was subtracted from any future earnings. In theory unlimited earnings were possible but only for those who were able or willing to work unlimited hours. As for the freedom, I failed to comprehend how being stuck in a small car with a frequently petrified new driver in any way constituted freedom. I did the training and stayed in the job for a couple of years. I eventually tried, unsuccessfully, to set up my own business with an acquaintance but ended up deep in debt after unwisely taking over a bank loan from my business partner but not the lease on the car it had been taken out for. After struggling along for a few months I eventually had to be bailed out by my father.

BRITISH AIRWAYS

Finally, a proper job. My career as a driving instructor had failed to give me the vast wealth I had thought it would. This was surely due to my lack of desire to work weekends and evenings, the time when most people want their lessons. I'd also had enough of living on cigarettes, Mars bars and Cornish pasties. I never found being a driving instructor stressful or dangerous: I just found it boring. So, when I saw an advert for *Reservations Sales Agents* to work for the national airline I leapt at the chance. The interviews seemed to go well but there was some doubt as to whether I could make the transition from fancy-free driving instructor to the apparently less exciting world of airline reservations. I had no doubt about my ability and succeeded in persuading the interviewer of the same. When I started work and met my fellow intake group, known as either 8/84 (designated by the month and year we started) or more realistically, by our colleagues, *The Addams Family (*a cruel and politically incorrect reference to the popular TV show about an oddball family) I realized what I had been competing against and why I had succeeded. I would have hated to see those who failed to be employed.

My bank manager was happy too. He didn't force me to close my account at least.

My career with *Britain's favourite airline*, as the marketing gurus had named it, lasted a few years. This wasn't my first exposure to the great unwashed, but it was certainly the first time I had contact, for 8 long hours a day, with the great unwashed travelling public.

'Do you fly to America?'

'What time is the last flight? OK, and what time is the one after that?'

'Can I take my dog on board?'

'I'm calling from the car (high tech in the early 80s), the traffic is terrible. Please hold the plane and I'll be there as soon as I can.'

What fun we had muting our little microphones and offering wonderfully acerbic answers such as,

'We do. Now, can you be just a bit more specific?'

'It's the LAST flight!'

'Only if he's dead.'

'Of course, I'm sure the other four hundred people on that flight won't mind.'

As Jean-Paul Sartre so nearly said, *Hell is other passengers*.

My linguistic genius meant that I earned an extra eight pounds a month and was occasionally called upon to speak German. I took a fairly basic test which I passed with ease and was allowed to wear a badge with a German flag on it. As I was a phone sales agent who never came into physical contact with customers this seemed rather pointless but I wore it with pride. Once or twice a week one of my colleagues would approach and tell me he or she had someone on a call who did not speak English but did speak German. I would rise to the occasion, literally rise as I had to walk over to whichever section of the vast hangar-like reservations centre they were located in, plug my tiny headset into their consul and say *Guten tag, wie kann ich Ihnen helfen?* This would invariably be followed by a frustrated German speaker wanting to change their flight on what was probably a non-changeable ticket. My usual response was to simply tell them they needed to take the ticket into one of the company's offices and have it checked by a ticket agent. Ticket agents were people far more qualified than us lowly reservations agents who could take responsibility for this type of complex transaction. They also got to wear a uniform.

There exists an important and complex hierarchy in an airline. Pilots are at the top of course, closely followed by cabin crew. During my time with British Airways, Concorde was operating and I imagine there was a special floor, gold key access only, built in the Ivory Tower for Concorde captains and crew. Next come the various engineering departments who made sure planes could take off, fly and land, preferably safely. These were followed by such obscure but exotically named sections as Avionics and Space Control. Moving down through the food chain we arrive at the people who were responsible for making the airline any money by ensuring customers bought tickets and actually travelled. Ticket office staff, who could be spilt into the sub-genres of airport and city, led the rally here closely followed by airport check-in teams. Beneath them, but always searching for a way to move up one rung and join the uniformed staff, came the reservations agents. We often operated in gloomy, dank conditions and at odd hours of the day, toiling endlessly and chained to our terminals: surely it was us who should be rewarded for our airlines' frequent Customer Service Awards. The only staff considered inferior to us were the sad individuals in accounts payable.

Most of the time I enjoyed my role and the occasional forays into translating strange travel terms such as *ticketed*, which became *geticketed*. This exciting feature of my mundane role inspired me to try learning another language so I started learning Italian. I'm still trying over 40 years later. I did this for two reasons: the company paid for the course and it meant that I was also asked to attend an internal training session entitled *Putting Yourself First*. People were selected for this training because they had shown initiative with their own development. Most of the other people attending were studying, in their own time, subjects far more important than mine, such an MBA or some other management diploma. My low key but valiant effort to better myself by attending a twice-a-week, hour-long beginners Italian course was not in the same league but it led to greater things that's for sure. And it's how I met my wife.

T worked in human resources and was attending the course as an observer to verify its content and effectiveness. Once the course finished we started seeing each other socially and eventually moved in together. We rented a small flat in Wraysbury, a quaint village near Heathrow airport. The flat was part of a bigger house owned by an eccentric couple who had lived there for years. There was quite a history attached to the house. It had originally been a monastery and was connected by an underground passage to the nearby church. Rumour had it that one of the brothers had been caught *in flagrante* with a visiting nun and walled up for his crime. It was a romantic spot, apart from the corralled monk, and we eventually got married there. T's mother was a bit surprised as, I found out later, she was convinced I was gay and only marrying her younger daughter for her money. She formed this opinion because I worked for an airline, had a moustache and I was still, at the age of 33, unmarried. T had been living in England for three years and had no desire to stay longer or experience another British winter. So we made plans to go to Australia.

AUSTRALIA TRIP TWO

Apart from familial ties I had no reason to stay in England and, having enjoyed my short stay there some years previously, was more than happy to emigrate to Australia. We flew to Sydney via Bangkok, Thailand where I would spend many a happy year later in my life.

The fun was just beginning; jobwise I was also lucky.

The world of the CRS (Computer Reservation System) was beginning to coalesce from the dust of various airlines. I was, for once in my life, in the right place at the right time. One of the three main CRS companies, Galileo, was hiring in Australia. Anyone, and I mean anyone, with any airline experience had a very good chance of getting in on the first floor of an illustrious career in a fledgling industry. One phone call and a quick interview in the pub later, I was hired as a *Support Executive*. Everyone was an executive in those days.

I spent two or three happy years with Galileo Australia as it later became known. I worked there much longer but was happy for only part of the time.

My support area was Cairns and the Gold Coast. Queensland's Cote d'Azur and Costa Brava rolled into one. Cruising the palm fringed streets, drinking coffee with travel agents and, just occasionally, loading some software or cleaning bits of sandwich off keyboards. It was a tough job, but somebody had to do it. Nothing good lasts forever and I felt I needed something more involving. Big mistake. The world of corporate sales beckoned and I rose to the challenge. More correctly I tripped and fell head first into a steaming pile of PowerPoint presentations. Wearing a suit in the sub-tropical heat was no fun. And all those early morning flights to Sydney and Melbourne... I yawn just thinking about it. I did amass a wonderful tie collection, however, which I still have to this day.

RETURN TO EUROPE

After eight years in Australia I began to miss the cultural diversity of Europe. Watching European movies and searching out German beer was one thing but I felt the need, more and more, to actually experience a European lifestyle for myself. Australia is a beautiful country but it is a long way from anywhere else. It's even a long way from other parts of Australia. I was putting on some red pants one morning when I had an epiphany. Time to return to Europe. Galileo's headquarters were in Swindon, a small and not overly interesting town west of London, and being based there did not appeal. I had heard of other CRS companies. One was called Amadeus and they had an office in the South of France! Now that was more like it. More palm trees and coffee but it wasn't two thousand miles to the next country. I looked at the map, Italy was right next door. Cappuccino. I enrolled on a French language course right away and sent off my resumé (it's French for CV you know).

I tried organising interviews remotely sending off my details and calling at odd times of the day but all to no avail. One day, after a particularly fraught day with the boss from hell I decided it was time to act. I contacted a travel agent friend of mine and arranged a one way ticket to Europe via Hong Kong. I travelled via Hong Kong as I had a contact there and I thought he might be able to help me find a job. It should have occurred to me that this was not likely to lead to anything much when he failed to show up to meet me at the airport as arranged.

So I travelled on to London where I half-heartedly followed up on a few options. I had no real desire to live or work in London again but I needed to start my *return to Europe* project somewhere. I knew a few people in Nice, France or more accurately, who worked in a large business park called Sophia Antipolis located near Nice. Low cost carriers were still in their infancy in 1997 so I bought a train ticket, at least not a bus this time, to Nice via Paris. On arrival I booked myself into a small hotel close to the head office of a well-known company and began pushing my skill-set to various interested parties. Some were more interested than others, it must be said.

Another new chapter in my life was about to begin. I liaised with one of the most helpful and considerate HR people I've ever met, who arranged a few interviews for me and I dutifully went through the motions. At one of these interviews something seemed to go right. Thierry had recently returned from a business trip to Australia and loved all things Australian. This was fortunate for me as I had an Australian passport. I accentuated my twang a little and threw in a few comments about Sydney Opera House and The Rocks. He seemed impressed and offered me the job. My role was never well defined. I think I was there to help Thierry document the various products and projects his team were involved in. The company was based in France but had a working language of English which, although everybody purported to speak the language, very few could write very well. But at least I was in. I stayed in Thierry's team for a while before moving to training.

I worked in Nice as a trainer for about eight years, travelling the world to such exotic places as Buenos Aires, Miami, Sydney and Crawley, developing and conducting training courses for our company's e-commerce products.

BANGKOK

When my wife was offered a role in Bangkok, Thailand I thought I should probably accompany her. We rented out our French apartment, arranged for our goods to be shipped to Bangkok and flew out to Asia. Life in Bangkok appealed to me. It's a crazy city but I've always thought that once you close your front door and the world is outside, it's not really important what goes on.

I had some health problems towards the end of my stay there. My story began with a spike, in more ways than one. An annual medical check showed increased PSA (a 'marker' in the blood that shows the level of a protein produced specifically by prostate cells) over a period of three years. The rubber gloves came out and I tried to relax as a man I hardly knew did what must be done. Not so bad, but I wouldn't recommend it as a life choice.

As advised by my doctor the next stage was a biopsy. This is done by inserting a probe in a place where the sun don't shine. I say probe, more like something Vlad the Impaler might once have used on his victims. If you gain nothing else from this please at least heed my advice: if ever you are unlucky enough to need to have this procedure done, insist on anaesthetic. Don't tough it out. If your doctor says you don't need anaesthetic, find another doctor because he is wrong, very wrong.

The implement used is not just a probe, oh no, it has a little gun on the end. The gun fires small metallic spears into you, grabs a lump or two of your precious prostate and removes them for examination. And it does this between ten and twenty times, each time more agonising than the last.

Then you wait a few days. You research all the reasons why your biopsy should not be found positive: no family history, not African American. You Google who's had prostate cancer, survived and gone on to greater things: Robert De Niro, Nelson Mandela, Laurence Olivier, Roger Moore, Ben Stiller, (who was only 46 when diagnosed. It's not just a disease for old guys). You try not to think about those who didn't. You try to carry on with your life as normal, except that now your identity has changed. Now you're *maybe I've got cancer guy*.

When I went back for the results I was still convinced I'd get the all clear. I couldn't be *cancer guy*. That wasn't me. That was something that happened to other people. In the doctor's office, pleasantries over, he opened the innocuous looking buff folder on his desk and I had the first inkling that the news wasn't going to be good. He wasn't smiling, the tissue box seemed to be closer to me than on previous visits, there was a nurse in the room. As he spoke I only heard odd words and phrases, *something there*, *malignant lesion*, *rogue cells* (What? There's a terrorist in my prostate).

I like to think I remained stoic. 'So what's next?' I asked in my best Martin Sheen as President Bartlett in *The West Wing* voice. The permacalm doc explained the options, none of which included what I wanted to hear 'only joking, you're fine', or 'wait a minute, I have the wrong file. This is for that other poor sucker who's got PROSTATE CANCER'.

It wasn't till I called my wife to tell her the news that it hit me and I started blubbering like a baby.

So what was next? My advice is simple: Check out ALL the options. See ALL the doctors. Get the BEST treatment you can afford.

After doing just that I opted for the wonderfully named robotic radical prostatectomy. Not scary sounding at all is it?

The days when handsome surgeons stood over their patient poking and prodding while concerned nurses wiped their brow are long gone, in the world of prostate surgery anyway. They use a robot now. Of course it's not the 70s *Danger Will Robinson*-type robot some of you may remember. This is a highly sophisticated piece of machinery which allows for far greater accuracy. And believe me, when you know what else is going on down there you really want accuracy.

Some weeks later though, as I lay on the slab calmed by drugs and beyond fear, I could not help but notice that the robot did somewhat resemble that fabulously neurotic tin can from *Lost in Space* and, what's more it was completely covered in some kind of cling film. I guess it needed protection to *boldly go where no-one (or robot) had gone before*.

I woke up a few hours later *aching in the places where I used to play* (L. Cohen) and with an excruciating pain in my shoulders. The human body is a strange thing. I was told the shoulder pain was due to having been tilted at a 45° angle, head down, for three hours, almost as long as a

Bruce Springsteen concert, so that the rock robot could Access All Areas. I didn't need to know anymore.

Life with no prostate is OK. For medical reasons, I now favour darker coloured trousers and I'm careful picking up my suitcase. Socially, I'm even more all mouth and no trousers with the ladies. And I guess I weigh a bit less.

But it's certainly better than being dead.

LEAVING BANGKOK

My wife had boarded her flight back to Australia following our few weeks together. I wandered aimlessly around the airport and settled back at the bar where we had shared a last drink before her flight departed.

I was still there some hours later staring into my empty coffee cup. *We close in five minutes. You'll have to leave.* One by one the lights flickered off. The cleaners had finally finished their repetitive and not overly effective mopping. Darkness had descended many hours previously and the vapour trails of the last departing flight had now merged with the sticky Bangkok night.

I was alone again. Alone in Bangkok. Alone at the airport and the last flight had left. In my self-absorbed and emotionally sensitive state I wondered, *Was it the last flight of the day or the last one ever?* I felt like those desperate souls must have years before, stranded on the roof of the US Embassy, attempting to flee as Saigon fell. A slight over dramatization, and of course, my situation was not quite so desperate but certainly I felt equally abandoned.

How had I ended up like this?

I'd arrived in Bangkok not long after my personal half-century for an extended stay in Asia. But, eight years can take its toll on anyone.

Workwise I'd had the not-uncommon internal political battles. Calling them battles gives them too much credibility. Perhaps feuds would be a better word.

There were also the aforementioned health problems which, although I had survived them relatively unscathed, had shaken me. In a perverse way they had also strengthened my resolve to move on. Certainly they had helped me put my life into perspective. *What doesn't kill you makes you stronger* apparently.

My domestic situation had changed some months previously when my wife had decided to leave Thailand and return to her native Australia to study.

I can remember the date, place and time when the novelty of this foreign posting had worn off. I was seated in my favourite bar, *Saucy Suzy*, on my favourite stool. I was sipping on a cold *Singha* beer and gazing pensively into the middle distance when it happened. I saw the reflection of an overweight, red-faced, wild-haired, sweaty guy and realized sadly that it was me. I was distraught. I knew that I had to leave. Not just the bar but Thailand.

Such were my thoughts as I stumbled out of the *Saucy Suzy*, bumping into a tall, slim woman who stroked my arm and said, *Hey sexy man, want to have some fun?* At least I think it was a woman. Fun was the last thing on my mind. As Bob Dylan famously said *Anyone can have fun, I just want to keep moving*.

I walked home slowly, sweat trickling down my back on another sultry Bangkok night, with the bass-heavy music emanating from every bar pounding in my head, thinking, *I gotta get out of this place, if it's the last thing I ever do.*

Falling in the front door of my apartment I added to my drunken state by gulping down a couple of shots before staggering into the bedroom and drifting into a drunken sleep.

I don't remember going to sleep but I do remember the lucid dream.

I was naked of course. A strong wind was blowing but I wasn't cold as I stood at the edge of the cliff. Looking down I could see a small house. As I flew down towards it I realized it wasn't a house but a whole town.

Once I'd landed I tried to walk towards a large glass building in the distance but my legs felt heavy and something kept holding me back. Fortunately there were rails alongside the road and I managed to drag myself towards the shiny office block at the end of it. Locating a door I tried to open it but was unsuccessful. No matter how hard I pushed, how hard I rang the bell, how hard I banged on the thick wood it refused to allow access. Fortunately this was a dream. As we all know you can do anything in a dream. So I simply walked through the door.

Once inside the building I became further disoriented. Corridors and passageways lead off in all directions. Elevators stopped at floors which did not exist. Eventually I found my office. All of my colleagues were sitting at their desks like corpses, heads down, headphones on, windows open. No-one seemed to notice me. I took a seat in a spare cubicle and switched on the PC. Strange symbols appeared on the screen. The keyboard was a pizza. I tried to use the phone but the cable was so entangled the whole desk lifted off the ground and disappeared. I tried to ask for help but everyone in the room had vanished.

The dream stayed with me the following day and for many days after that. I saw it as an omen that I needed to double my efforts to return to Europe. Inwardly I was torn. I loved living in Thailand but I knew I had to be practical about my future.

THE FINAL YEARS IN FRANCE

I t took a while but I was finally successful in moving back to France. I'd been applying for various jobs for a number of months with no success. Occasionally I would receive a reply and possibly even arrange an interview but then, nothing. This didn't surprise me. I was nearing sixty and despite their claims of cultural, gender and age equality, I knew that anyone looking at my CV would soon realize my advanced years, while ignoring my vast experience, and take no further interest. Fortunately I had a friend, Peter, who was a director at my company's head office and, as he was visiting Bangkok for a conference we arranged to meet.

Normally of course I would have met him at the office or gone to whichever hotel he was staying in but unfortunately I'd just come out of hospital that day, following some minor neck surgery. I didn't feel up to bouncing through the Bangkok night to where the company's office was located in a Thai taxi or on the back of a motor bike. Peter graciously offered to meet somewhere a bit closer to where I lived. So we met in a bar near my little apartment.

I mentioned that I'd had neck surgery and I was a bit self-conscious about the large bandage that was covering an area of my neck recently explored by the surgeon's knife. In an attempt to cover it I decided to wear a little scarf like a cravat around my neck.

Peter thought this hilarious, or ridiculous, I'm not sure which, but he seemed impressed with something and suggested I meet with other members of his management team to pursue the options, which I duly did and a few months later my return to France was complete.

OTHER JOURNEYS

COMMUTING – LONDON

I've had, in the words of all the great writers, heaps of jobs. Some better than others, ranging from stultifying in the extreme through boring to vaguely challenging but I'd still rather be doing something else. Like most of us I envy those who feel they are spending their working lives doing their true calling, or passion – rock stars, astronauts, those helping the sick and needy. For me the daily drudge has never been what gets me out of bed in the morning. Regardless of what might happen once I arrive, the best part of any workday is the journey to work, especially when it's possible to do it on foot. Lengthy commutes in crowded trains or heaving buses are no fun for anyone but the times when I have been able to walk, or at least take a short public transport journey and then walk, have always been the best. Of the many years I spent in various badly paid and under achieving employment in London I would always search out the most interesting routes to my place of employment.

During my tenure with the now defunct Niagara Finance in Oxford Street I lived in a variety of scungy bedsits and shared houses in the less popular – in those days at least – parts of London. From these badly ventilated, noisily plumbed dens I would set off each morning and after a few days of taking the most obvious, direct route by bus or train I would start to work out more interesting routes. Getting to Oxford Street from any suburb offered a plethora of choices.

For a while I lived in Wimbledon. Often I would take the district line tube, changing to the Piccadilly line at Barons Court (never Earls Court where all the tourists would change) and then alight at Piccadilly itself, unable to bear more marching myrmecomorphically underground to take the one stop up to Oxford Circus, the closest stop to my place of work. From here an early morning – it was always early – stroll along Regent Street before cutting through to Carnaby Street and Soho. This was in the mid-70s and Carnaby Street was no longer quite as fashionable as it had been in its 60s' heyday but I still felt a twinge of excitement as I walked its hallowed pavement.

COMMUTING – WALTROP, GERMANY

O r as it was called back then, West Germany.
Thanks to my father's high-level connections
with the council – he was the treasurer, mainly
because no-one else wanted the job and the fact that
Herne Bay was twinned with the small German town of
Waltrop in NordRhein-Westfalen – I landed a job, a few
jobs in fact, in the industrial heartland of Germany. I lived
in the country for a year or so, gainfully employed as a *Gas-
tarbeiter*, a somewhat derogatory term for a foreign worker.
My first job very nearly killed me. I spent those weeks
working as a labourer on a building site. Not something I
was ever really cut out to do. Manual labour was not then
and is not now, my forté. Apart from the working day
being 06:00 to 17:45 every day with fifteen minutes for
breakfast and thirty for lunch it also involved a 15 kilometre commute, which, thanks to my being unable to
afford a car when I arrived, I did by bike. Timing is everything and I well remember setting my alarm clock for
04:50 when I would roll out of bed, pull on my clothes and
stumble, bleary eyed, out to the garage of the house where

a borrowed bike was kept. For a while I used a moped, also borrowed, but there was a problem with the motor and I spent most of the time pedalling it to keep moving anyway.

I was lodging with a formidable German widow and her amiable 18-year-old son, Klaus. After a day of hard labour I'd cycle home again, eat whatever potato based meal Frau Niestadtkoetter had prepared, drag myself upstairs to my small room and fall into bed. I suppose I must have showered now and then but I don't remember. I lasted only a few weeks in the job before taking up employment in a local factory. Not exactly a better job but at least I only had to work eight hours a day and I could take a bus. The downside, one of many in retrospect, was that the job involved shift work. I realized I was also was not designed to work at night or indeed at any time much after five-thirty in the evening. This experience also earned the distinction of it being the first and only time I was ever sacked from a job. This came about after a particularly strenuous night of moving piles of treated metal from one corner of the warehouse to another when I lay down on a bench and promptly fell asleep. I learnt from the experience that I'm a morning person and that if you are going to fall asleep at work don't do it five minutes before the boss arrives.

COMMUTING – COPENHAGEN

I n the early 80s I found myself working in the Danish capital for a year or so. I was employed as a houseman in a large hotel. Houseman was a local term, anywhere else it would just be porter or maybe concierge. It wasn't the best job I'd ever had, nor was it the worst and it was one step up from being a maid or whatever the male term for that may be. I lived with a gay friend of mine a little way down one of the main streets of Copenhagen, Vesterbrogade. The hotel was a little way out of town and was, during my tenure, the main airport hotel. It wasn't particularly close to the airport but it was situated on the same small island, Amager. These days there's a direct train from the city centre to the airport which then continues on via bridge and tunnel all the way to Sweden. But back in 1981 the number 42 bus was the way to go – in fact it was the only way. I didn't live on that route so I had to take another bus from my street to the main square or Rådhuspladsen and connect to the 42 which passed the hotel. After a few weeks of jumping on and off buses, frequently falling over on the icy streets and tiring of just missing a connection and having to wait on the windswept street corners of Hans Christian Andersen's hometown, I realized that it was more practical to walk the whole way. It was a great opportunity to explore the backstreets of Copenhagen and it kept me from freezing to death at bus stops. I discovered a particularly interesting route which took me along the slightly seedy street of Istegade, around the back of the main station – always an interesting area in any city – and then across a small bridge where there was simply no escaping the bitter easterly wind whipping off the Baltic. Having completed the bridge crossing I then hunched my shoulders against the cold and walked the last few hundred yards, head down and dreaming, to the staff entrance of the hotel and into the relative warmth. As my shared accommodation had no central heating this would be the first time of the day that I was warm. And I relished the feeling. I marvel now that I was ever able to leave the comfort of my bed.

COMMUTING – BRISBANE

J ust before moving to France from Australia in 1997 I started a new job with a well-known hotel chain. This career move coincided with a physical move from the countryside south of the city to an apartment in an inner-city suburb, close enough to walk to work. As had happened before in my illustrious career, the job itself didn't work out for a number of reasons, the main one being my evil boss. She seemed to lack any sense of humanity or interest for those in her charge. My every action was questioned, my suggestions ignored or stolen. As each day in the office became more and more unbearable my only pleasure came from the forty minute or so walk through Brisbane's South Bank complex and along the Queen Street mall to the office situated in Post Office Square. Most days I walked home as well stopping off for a beer at one of the many river front bars along the way. It was uphill going home so I felt the beer was justified. Some days, had it been possible, I would have stopped for a beer on the way in to work as well even though it was downhill all the way, in more ways than one.

COMMUTING – BANGKOK

I spent eight years in Bangkok, most of them pretty happy times. The last three of these I lived in a serviced apartment in the infamous Nana area, also known as *Soi 4*. A *soi* is simply a small street or alley leading off the main *thanon* or road. Often, surely just to baffle foreigners, one *soi* will lead off another *soi* which is very confusing. When people asked me where I lived I would simply say, *a Soi off Sukhumvit*. Sukhumvit is the main Bangkok artery running right through the centre of the city and eventually all the way to the Cambodian border. *Which one?* they would ask innocently, and when I replied *Soi 4* they would react in one of two ways: a knowing smile or an embarrassed laugh. In fact, while *Soi 4* did play host to a number of seedy establishments offering the kind of entertainment for which Bangkok is well known, it also had its cultural side. Like all the best football matches, the road was really a *soi* of two halves. The top end nearest to Sukhumvit was the place for late night revellers. But venture further down and it became a very pleasant, quite leafy residential area where there was a primary school and a number of perfectly lovely restaurants. Not to say that the frisson of walking down the *soi* on my way home from work in the early evening was not in itself an experience. Equally so, on occasions I would be taking a moped taxi to work around 07:30 and it would not be unusual to come across a group of staggering drunkards still hoping to find some action.

2018

LA VITA NUOVA

3 1 July 2018 was the day I retired: it was a Tuesday. Finally, free from the shackles of commerce, I would be at liberty to pursue the plan I had been thinking about for quite a while. It had long been my intention to relive at least part of my ill-fated tandem adventure exactly 40 years after the first escapade. Circumstances beyond my control prevented that but during 2018 I was at last ready to make a start. Being older and, I like to think, if only slightly, wiser, I was not so foolish or naïve as to imagine for a moment that I could at this stage of my life ride any kind of normal bike from Enfield to Athens, or really any small part of it. On a recent trip to Thailand I had assumed there was some problem with my borrowed bike as I tried to accompany my wife and friends to the village shop. Either that or an elephant was trying to hitch a ride.

Fortunately here in the present, which is now the future, an array of hi-tech equipment is at my disposal: GPS, mobile phones, Facetime and most important of all, the wonder of the electric bike. It's hard for me to over-state the advantage of this technology. No longer is it necessary to pant and sweat on long, seemingly unending hills. Or to grimace and curse as the wind changes direction yet again and begins to blow from whichever direction I have decided to pedal in. Cycling puritans decry the e-bike. Let them. I'd suffered enough, it was time to have some fun.

TO CAMP OR NOT

Accommodation was something else I happily upgraded for the later trip. On the initial expedition Alan and I started out treating ourselves to official camp sites. These were plentiful and relatively cheap in France. Showers, toilets, even a little shop where we could spend more than our budget allowed on chocolate bars. Soon we realized that we really didn't need, and certainly could not afford, all these luxuries on anything approaching a daily basis. We were on a budget tighter than Pavarotti's waistband. Financial geniuses that we were we calculated we could save a fortune by only luxuriating in the tepid showers of a *camping* once or twice a week. On all other occasions we would simply find a quiet field in which to erect our bright orange tent and pass the night. On one memorable occasion we passed the night on a rubbish tip. Sure, now and then a farmer would come to check us out, a wild animal might sniff around but, generally our nights passed peacefully. Once we crossed into Italy, where campsites became more expensive, we pretty much gave up on the luxury of an official sleeping place altogether and spent most nights hidden away, as much as you can be hidden in an orange tent, in vineyards or behind rubbish tips. Any piece of flat dry ground would suffice. Some were definitely flatter and drier than others.

40+ YEARS ON

There are many differences between the ethos of a 21 year old and that of a 63 year old. In my mind I'm still the same person, full of dreams and fantasies, many of them surprisingly, some might say sadly, the same as those I had at 21. This despite, or perhaps because of, my favourite Henry Miller line *I have no money, no hopes, no resources, I am the happiest man alive.*

I have more money now without a doubt. Back in 1976 I was just a dreamer, no plans outside of living. Imagining what might happen more than a week or so ahead was beyond me. As we grow older we become more aware of our actions and how they might affect our ever diminishing future. At the age of 21 I barely considered my life beyond the next sandwich. Not in any practical sense anyway. Sure, I had dreams of travelling to exotic places, meeting strange and wonderful people, maybe even falling in love. I have some vague recollection of wanting this to be with a Polish girl in Tibet, for reasons which escape me now but I'm sure it made sense at the time. But in any real sense of the word I had no idea as to how my future might turn out. Quite how I thought a badly planned, ill-executed cycling jaunt through off-season Europe would help me towards a more useful future I have no idea but somehow I knew it would.

DELIVERY AND COLLECTION

A few months before the auspicious day of my retirement I had shipped my brother's bicycle, a German made Kalkhoff, from the UK to France and arranged to have the battery replaced. Three years unattended in a cold garage had long depleted any power it had to the extent that it was also beyond recharging. I found a helpful local expert in a bike shop in Nice where I ordered a new battery and I was finally ready to go.

My first ride was from the shop in Nice back to my apartment 20 kilometres or so down the coast. I collected the bike on a busy Saturday afternoon and set off into the city traffic. At first the bike seemed heavy and I realized that, so keen had I been to get going, I had forgotten to activate the electronic motor so I was in fact simply riding a heavy bike with no assistance whatsoever. Even so I recall, it was still easier to move and manoeuvre than the tandem had been. I pulled over and switched on the power. What a difference. I glided through the jostling, fuming cars and headed for the coast. Once on the Promenade des Anglais, the main coastal strip which passes through Nice, I manoeuvred my way around the late season visitors and continued easily along the coast road. The ride on the flat was enjoyable but it wasn't until I headed inland towards my rented apartment and hit the hills that I appreciated the advantage of the technology beneath me. A slight increase in the power of my pedalling and I felt like Superman newly arrived from planet Krypton. I was almost flying up hills which, on a standard bike, would have had me huffing, puffing and sweating like a huffy, puffy sweaty thing. I didn't even need a shower when I got home. But I had one anyway. And a beer.

E-COMMUTE

I began familiarising myself with the bike, and the feel of riding an e-bike, by making a few short forays around the local area and riding to work. This proved to be quicker than driving most days as I passed crawling cars, which for the most part contained just a frustrated driver and, now and then, a bored looking passenger. On my first morning I succumbed to over confidence and made the mistake of trying to find a shortcut, which resulted in me becoming hopelessly lost two kilometres from my house, and less than one from my destination. My innate sense of direction prevailed and after negotiating a stretch of wasteland and a few housing estates, which I didn't even know existed, I eventually found my way back to the main road. Needless to say, the shortcut I had followed and which eventually led me back on to my original route, came out about fifty metres along the road I would have been on had I not strayed from my planned route. But it didn't matter and despite the extra distance, a sense of adventure and achievement remained. Upon arriving at the office on that first morning it was gratifying to see how many of my colleagues also used electric bikes as part of their daily commute. I was not alone. I managed to continue riding to and from work for a couple of months before it became too cold and dark.

By the following year we had moved to another location further from where I was working. Undaunted, I intended to continue riding at least once a week. My resolve soon faded and my commute by bike dwindled to once a month. It was an enjoyable ride for the most part, along the coast towards the resort town of Cannes and then inland via a combination of cycle paths and main roads to the office which was located in a business park situated in the hills behind the city. One would think that the most enjoyable part of the journey would be through the glamorous town of Cannes, but this was not the case. Many towns and cities look their best at six-thirty in the morning. Traffic is light and as dawn rises the feel of a place awakening to face the day is palpable. Not Cannes, or at least not the part I rode through. Each morning I would have to navigate my way around trucks servicing the big hotels along the promenade and avoid all manner of council workers busily employed maintaining the film resort's sheen by cutting down overgrown palm trees. The sprinklers always seemed to be on, wasting valuable water, to keep all the grass a bright shade of green. They invariably flooded the road and, combined with delivery trucks, created an obstacle course of puddles, especially where the sprinklers were badly maintained and were spraying more water on the road than on the grass.

EXTRAS

Riding the few kilometres to work each morning was hardly an expedition but it gave me a taste of the thrills to come. As I became more familiar with the bike I began to investigate other trips that I might make further afield. These included repeating a ride from just across the border with Italy and extended to dreaming of a ride to Rome. I spent hours, when I should have been working, accessing numerous websites and poring over routes along with places to stay and visit. I also spent more time and money than I should have purchasing little extras to make my riding that bit more perfect. Numerous articles of clothing along with safety devices, including an alarm which gave off an ear-piercing shriek if anybody tried to move the bike without my permission, and the constant, ultimately futile, search for that perfect saddle. And one or two other essential purchases too, such as a Bluetooth speaker for music while I rode.

ACROSS THE BORDER

Another short trip I did to get myself used to being back in the saddle was with my wife Tracy, from our summer retreat in Mandelieu across the border into Italy. We travelled by train from our apartment to Ventimiglia, just over the Italian border, and spent a pleasant couple of days riding along the Italian coast on a newly constructed bike track where the old railway line used to be.

Our days in Italy were pleasant but uneventful. The fun started on our way home. We rode back as far as Ventimiglia along a lovely path which ran adjacent to the coast for most of the way before hitting the Ventimiglia traffic and battling our way to the station. Tracy waited outside guarding the bikes while I went in to buy tickets. We had around forty minutes before the next train so all seemed good.

But the situation changed when, upon entering the ticket hall I was immediately faced with one of those decisions you just know is going to take you down a path you do not wish to go. My dichotomy? Use the automatic machines, or join the relatively short queue and practise my limited Italian with the two typically Italian looking staff? One a portly gentleman with a slightly bored countenance, the other a late blooming punk lady of around forty-five with a stud in her chin. I figured I had already used most of my Italian word allowance for that day and went for the machines. All seemed well as I worked my way through the numerous options of the touchscreen – language, destination, date and time of travel, number of passengers, select train. And this is where the problems started; *train selected not available for purchase.* Well, to quote Richard Branson, *Why the fu**ing hell not?* But no matter how vehemently I chided the shiny glass screen it refused to change its mind and deliver.

Defeated once again by machinery, I returned to the now lengthier queue to practise my linguistic skills. As I stood patiently waiting the time ticked by. Forty minutes had already become thirty while I was battling with the errant technology of the automatic machine. Now it passed again as my fellow passengers quizzed the two, in my opinion far too helpful, ticket salespeople. *Just buy a ticket somewhere. What are you doing? Ordering a pizza, asking which wine will best complement your panini, discussing the Pope's dress sense?*

Time continued its inexorable march. I finally arrived at the ticket counter with around 10 minutes to spare, *due per Antibes* I said smiling. Buttons pushed, tickets began slowly printing. Total cost 20.80 euros and of course all my change and credit cards were with the bike so I handed over two 20 euro notes. Punk lady looked a little peeved but began slowly counting out change. This of course necessitated the opening of numerous small packets of coins and carefully placing them in the correct compartment of her antiquated till. Finally, tickets in hand, I rushed out to collect the bikes and a by-now-somewhat-concerned wife (naturally I had left my phone outside as well so had no way to tell her the cause of my delay). She had assumed digestion issues.

We raced to the platform, arriving at the bottom of the access stairs at just the same time as two young Italian girls who had chosen this exact spot to study the departures board, for, what I can only assume, was a test of some kind they intended to take later. I hate being rude but knowing we had about 30 seconds to board I simply pushed my bike straight at them in a non-characteristically aggressive fashion and they scurried away. I felt guilty but empowered as I heaved my bike up the stairs and onto the train. We took our seats and sat in quiet reflection for at least five more minutes before the train finally departed.

LYON TO MANDELIEU – STRIKE 1

On the original trip Alan and I had not covered the stretch between Lyon and the Riviera by bike having decided it all looked very hilly so we took a train. If I remember correctly two trains; one from Lyon to Marseilles where we spent the night sleeping on the station platform, and the following morning connecting through to Nice. We could have stayed on that train as it terminated in Ventimiglia Italy, as it still does today, but we thought we should at least cross the French–Italian border on the bike. I assume our arrival in Nice, only 30 kilometres or so from the Italian border, was late in the afternoon because we decided to spend another night in France before the exciting prospect of crossing into a new country. Open, flat ground to pitch a tent was hard to find on the precipitous cliffs of the lower corniche. We pedalled along trying to enjoy the spectacular views while at the same time hoping to pass a suitable camping zone. As night fell we realized we would have to be inventive. We had no lights (of course) and even we were wary of riding in the growing dusk along such a road. Just before it grew completely dark we spotted a small area just off the road which looked reasonably secluded. Having little choice, we decided to spend the night there. There was no space to erect the tent so we simply huddled up in our sleeping bags and quickly fell into our normal exhausted sleep. The night passed uneventfully and it was only as the dawn light glistened off the Mediterranean that we realized we had camped on yet another rubbish tip.

The plan for the repeat journey was to take the train again, but this time in the opposite direction, from the coast to Lyon and then spend a leisurely few days riding back home. But fate had other plans. A few weeks before our planned departure the French train unions decided they hadn't had a strike for a while and that early spring would be a good time. But in France they don't just strike for a day or two – they take it seriously.

SNCF drivers planned strikes over a three-month period, two days in every five. And of course, to cause maximum disruption, they were frequently scheduled on weekends. It was hard to sympathise with their plight. French train drivers have a job for life, get automatic pay rises and can retire at age fifty-two. Sitting President Macron wanted to make some changes to that for new employees and the unions were not happy. As a colleague of mine said, *It's not like they're shovelling coal anymore*. He also said a few other things which are best not repeated.

I had no choice but to implement a workaround. As Plato said, *Necessity is the mother of invention*. My many years of working with computer software engineers had given me a massive amount of experience in the area of workarounds. Engineers, who seldom actually deal with customers at all, indeed I doubt they have any real idea that someone might ever actually use the product they are dreaming up, seem to think that whatever can be done with their code should be done. Unfortunately, their failure to understand that most consumers care more about the functions and features that they actually use, and not the things that some weed smoking, coffee guzzling fantasist has dreamt up, makes life a challenge for anyone who can converse in complete sentences and doesn't always wear a T-shirt to work. The fact that by selecting some special option your computer you can suddenly contact aliens is not really relevant if you don't care about contacting aliens. My workaround was simple enough, I would move my departure date by one day, avoid the striking train drivers and give myself an extra day to complete the trip.

The rescheduling of the first day proved to be futile. A couple of weeks before departure a second obstacle raised its head. Like some celestial warning that I was not as young as I used to be, my back went into spasm one morning as I was about to wash my face. It was an interesting experience. One minute all was well and the next I simply could not move. Bad as this would have been the situation was exacerbated by my being home alone, my wife having taken a short trip to London. After around thirty minutes of agony and immobility, I did manage to stagger back into my bedroom and eventually – but it took some time – I fell onto the bed and into relative comfort. But what now? Being virtually incapacitated is a strange experience. I considered my options: 1. Call an ambulance. 2. Stagger to my neighbours' place and ask them to call an ambulance. (I decided against this option mainly because I was only wearing my underpants and I really didn't know them that well.) 3. Wait a bit and hope things improved. I went for option three of course and a few hours later was able to move a little more.

A few days later, limited mobility was achieved and I started wondering how I was still going to complete the first part of trip. The doctor had prescribed pain medication but after only two days of taking whatever concoction he thought best, I began having an unpleasant reaction. Exhaustion set in along with a fever and the firm belief that I was near to death. The doctor changed my medication and my situation improved gradually over the next couple of days. As did my resolve to lose weight and exercise more.

I stretched and exercised as much as I could in the following few days and, by the time the intended date of departure came around, I was cycling fit once again. But we still had the train strike situation to contend with. Finally, we decided to delay the Lyon–Mandelieu stage until trains were running normally, whenever that might be, and just to head off from our apartment into the Var, a pleasant rural region to the west of Mandelieu. That way we could pace ourselves and, should any major disaster befall either of us, we would not be more than a day or two from home. This was not the adventurous, carefree trip I had conceived months before. In fact, if anything it proved – if proof were needed – that my attitude to travel had changed quite dramatically from the days of my youth.

DAY 1

The night before departure, to celebrate my having ten days off work, much wine and other alcoholic beverages were consumed. This resulted in a slightly later start than planned. And, despite meticulous planning and packing for many days prior, I realized just as we were finally about to get rolling that I had not packed any long trousers for evening wear. It was still only late April and years of living in tropical climates had made me something of a weakling when it came to feeling the cold. I hurriedly rushed upstairs to pack the extra garment, and we finally departed. We headed west along the coast road towards Frejus.

It was a beautiful morning and the road was busy with cars and other cyclists, mostly in groups, all of whom seemed to be competing to go faster than each other. I've never understood the attraction of cycling as a team event. For me it's the perfect opportunity for some silent contemplation as the rhythmic motion of rubber on tarmac propels you along. But for some it's a head down, push as hard as you can battle to make it to the invisible finish line before the other guy. For me the best part of cycling is when you stop. Dismounting in a quiet spot along the way and listening to your own heartbeat and the gentle sounds of nature is one of the best things about the sport.

We arrived at our hotel in St Maxime ahead of schedule and checked in before riding into town where we had lunch at a café where the unnecessary music was playing just within the borders of annoyance. After lunch we decided to continue along the coast to the fabled town of St Tropez. I'm not sure why. There was a well laid bike track all the way which made the ride itself pleasurable enough. But St Tropez itself, really what's the point? I'm sure back in its 60s' heyday when it was a lovely hidden beach village, frequented by the rich and famous, it was a place to aspire to. And it is in a beautiful location. Now, I think like so many places in the world, it looks gorgeous from a distance but come too close and you'll see the scars. We rode around town for a bit yacht spotting before heading back to the bike track and our hotel for the night.

DAY 2

Our plans for this few days exploratory trip, never more than vague, remained loose. We decided to head for a small village we knew, where I had stayed on another cycling jaunt a few years previously, called Sillans La Cascade. I was already quite familiar with the range and power of my bike but my wife was still in the throes of discovering how far she could ride before the battery went flat and she was left to ride a heavy bike with no assistance. We had had some experience of this situation the previous day when we decided to leave the bike batteries charging while we rode the few kilometres into town for lunch. The first kilometre was uneventful especially as it was downhill but when we reached the undulating coast road we realized our folly. We persevered and pedalled our way to the nearest restaurant we could find. As we ate and attempted conversation above the music both of us were unable to dispel thoughts of what the ride back uphill would be like with no assistance. We slept well that night.

DAY 3

The next day dawned with the threat of rain. Undaunted, and with our batteries fully charged, we headed north in the direction of Sillans. Almost immediately the road started climbing. With electric bikes hills are less of a physical challenge, but they do deplete the power of the battery more quickly. This is an immutable law of physics. We'd only been riding for an hour or so when my wife announced that she was *down to two bars*. No way would we make Sillans today. Still we pedalled on in the hope of finding a friendly bar owner who would allow us to recharge the batteries. As we rounded yet another precipitous turn we found just such a place. A service station with bar attached. In we went and, over the noise of the raucous locals, who were drinking beer from wine glasses, asked if we could plug in and literally recharge our batteries. No problem, replied the friendly harridan behind the bar. The bar was actually quite large but, as we wanted to remain close to our recharging batteries lest some wayward local decided he could put them to better use, we ensconced ourselves at a table right next to the bar itself, where the locals were engaged in some kind of shouting match punctuated by loud cries of *yaaa* every few seconds. We sipped our bitter coffee and tried to write in our journals, conversation was futile. Slowly, one by one the blue lights of our batteries flickered on and after an hour or so we felt ready to leave. Coincidentally just as we paid the bill and reconnected our power source to the bikes all the locals decided it was time to leave as well. It was around 11:45 and I assume lunchtime for them. Their Sunday morning carousing was over for another week. None of them seemed to be on foot so we waited a little longer before continuing on our way, hoping we would not need to share the road with any of the well refreshed natives as they meandered home in their ancient and battered Peugeots and Renaults.

We never did make it to Sillans. After a few more hours of riding through pleasant countryside we pitched up at a small town called Lorgues. Batteries were again close to flat and we decided to spend the night. I found us a place to stay via my favourite hotel booking app and we headed there to check in. On arrival the place was deserted. I called the phone number provided and a friendly sounding lady called Florence invited me to leave a message. It was then that I looked more closely at the confirmation on my phone, check-in between 18:00 and 19:00. It was around three in the afternoon and the prospect of standing outside Florence's *gite* for three hours in the misty rain did not appeal. I cancelled the booking and we headed back into town with the intention of staying in a solid looking but probably expensive hotel we had spotted earlier.

On the way back in to town we noticed another sign for accommodation and once again I called the number. The lady who answered seemed surprised that we should just show up but was happy to let us see what was available.

My heart beat a little more joyfully as she led us through the gate to her palatial looking home. We headed for a wonderfully large chalet type arrangement which had a living room with separate bedroom and bathroom. Disappointingly the accommodation on offer was just the rather cramped bedroom and what was described as an Italian bathroom. 'Yes, very big' said our hostess mischievously. Rain had started to fall more heavily and neither of us wanted to remount and pedal on – the hotel in town might well be full anyway. So I begrudgingly handed over the princely sum of 70 euros in exchange for the key. It was only later as we squeezed ourselves in to the small room and started to try and unpack that we realized, not only had we paid far too much for what was really very basic accommodation, but also that she had forgotten to give us any towels. We showered, both using as much hot water as humanly possible in an effort to get our money's worth and dried ourselves on our dirty clothes then watched a movie on my phone before settling down to try and sleep in what must have at some stage been a teenager's bedroom. The large living room with flat screen TV and comfortable sofa was tantalisingly close and clearly visible through a locked glass door. We did some washing and dried it by leaving the heated towel rail in the Italian bathroom on all night. Retribution of a kind we thought. It rained heavily until the early hours of the morning.

The night in the Lilliputian room reminded me that there comes a stage in life when you realize that travel is all very well but really, being at home is not so bad. As a young man of course all I wanted to do was travel, be it overland to India or simply taking the bus to London for the weekend. I wanted to be on the move. The stultified life I led in my small English coastal town and later on in various depressing bedsits and overcrowded flats in the cheaper suburbs of London was something I wanted to escape from. Who wouldn't? And as I got older and started to travel for work it all seemed so exotic: Hilton and Marriott hotels, endless hot water, a TV in my room, business class flights – I was living the dream. But soon I came to realize that travelling for work is not as glamorous as it seems. Sure, I saw places I would probably never have seen and my first few business class flights made me feel special but after a while even that paled. I could sit at home and watch a movie in a comfortable chair drinking fine wine and not have to worry about immigration lines and finding a taxi to my hotel when I arrived.

DAY 4

Following our uncomfortable night in the doll's house we both decided we should head home. We could easily make it in a day and then we would be back in our own comfortable apartment and not worrying about our saddles getting wet. It was a cop out to be sure but we felt we had made a start and had come to know our bikes and our own limitations a little better. We found our way back to the coast road and joined the throngs heading for Cannes and Nice.

ITALY AGAIN

After a day or two resting up and getting a few repairs done to my bike we decided to head off again. The plan was to take a train across the border to Italy, something we had done many times previously. I often thought that one of the best things about living in the south of France was that Italy was so close. We'd avoid navigating our way through Monaco with its extensive network of tunnels and then ride to the charming seaside town of Alassio. But SNCF were still striking – at least they were consistent – and two more days of dubious train schedules loomed. And the weather was not looking good. After minimal deliberation we decided to drive the eighty or so kilometres, intending to hire bikes on arrival. But we never did. Once we'd arrived in the quaint town of Alassio and checked in to a lovely little bed and breakfast which was, somewhat ironically as it turned out, directly opposite a bicycle hire shop, our enthusiasm faded. It was wet and windy, not ideal conditions for cycling, but perfect for sitting in bars quaffing Chianti. But, more than that, the idea of exploring the town and environs on rented bicycles simply did not appeal. Rented bikes are always too small for anyone over six feet tall except, I would assume, in Holland where the tallest people in Europe live. So, we walked around a bit, ate some delicious pasta, drank some delicious wine and enjoyed some pleasant walks along the beach. Our few days across the border passed uneventfully and we arrived back in France loaded up with Italian wine, cheese and olive oil.

What this short sojourn in Italy did inspire us to do was to completely rethink the original plan to ride from Calais to Lyon retracing the trip I had done on the rusting Raleigh some forty years previously. It was a plan fraught with complications in the first place. My bike was too large to easily fit in our small French car, certainly without removing both wheels and all other protuberances. Removing items tends to be fairly simple, reattaching them often is not. I had checked the train options but, in addition to the planned strikes, which showed no sign of abating and were scheduled to run on through to the end of July, there was also the fact that, unlike forty years previously when it was possible to pretty much turn up at a station, buy a ticket and board any train, these days, with the advent of the TGV, one has to book in advance. Also due to some inexplicable law, presumably one of the few which was not laid down hundreds of years ago during the Napoleonic period and never rescinded, bikes were only allowed on trains bound for or departing from, Paris. The illogicality of this situation reminded me of the farcical *priorite a droit* which stipulates that the clapped-out Citroen, emerging from the tiniest side road imaginable, has right of way over any vehicle on the main road. Back in the 1800s presumably this law made sense. When locals were conveying themselves in horse and carts, those who were descending from the hilltop villages, often wealthy landowners who found it hard to slow down, expected the vehicles on the flat, with a better view, to decrease speed and allow them to merge safely onto the main road. One assumes that failure to do so, apart from resulting in an injured horse or two, might also mean that poor Pierre would not only lose his hay, but also possibly his head.

Now it simply causes more accidents and ill feeling than anything apart from perhaps drink–driving and texting.

All of these complications led us to forget the Calais to Lyon plan and instead take a two-week ride from our still relatively undiscovered French haven of Mandelieu along the Ligurian coast in the direction of Rome. Still avoiding Monaco of course by finding a day when strikes were not planned (the ever thoughtful SNCF had published a detailed schedule of when strikes would take place) and taking the train to Ventimiglia. Early morning cappuccinos were assured. This plan ticked a few other boxes as well. Back in the seventies my pal Alan and I had done nothing more than ride across the border to the first Italian town of Ventimiglia and then, as you might remember, board another train straight to Rome, in search of the ever-elusive spare parts. Now accompanied by my wife I intended to cover that missing part of the original itinerary by bike. The plan was to cycle all the way to Rome although we soon realized that was beyond our physical capabilities. Pasta, wine and gelato beckoned, and it would, we assumed, be warmer than Northern France too.

MANDELIEU TO LEVANTO, ITALY

P lanning around the continuing SNCF train strikes we left on a Friday morning from our apartment to take the short ride to Cannes la Bocca and then the train across the border to Ventimiglia in Italy. French trains run on a very obscure timetable and on the day we left there was no direct train from Mandelieu to Ventimiglia, so we needed to start with a relatively short five kilometre ride to the nearest serviced station. All packed, and with our bikes loaded, we were about to set off when I realized I did not have the key to my battery lock. Being unable to remove the battery would make life very difficult, if not impossible. Charging it would mean using a very long extension cord. I didn't possess such a thing and, even if I did, I did not relish the idea of carrying it with me. I began to search for the errant key. As one does when an item is mislaid I looked in all the obvious places, then I started looking in all the less obvious places. I searched manically in drawers I had not opened for months, shorts I could never remember cycling in. I squatted low on the bathroom floor in case I had somehow dropped the key there. My wife helped and between us we discovered any number of old keys, none of which had anything to do with my bike. Time was running out, we had to leave for the station or face missing the train and, due to the vagaries of the coastal timetable, waiting around two hours for the next one. Bags were upturned, old paint pots shuffled around and various items, which had been stored in our garage for years, moved in a futile search for the errant key. I began to lose hope and wondered if we might have to resort to abandoning the ride altogether, when suddenly my addled brain connected a few extra synapses and finally remembered that I had stored the keys in a small compartment in the saddle-bag of my bike. I unzipped the small pocket and there, glistening in the morning sunlight were my keys.

Panic over. Let the trip begin.

SAN REMO TO ALBENGA

The short ride to Cannes La Bocca station was uneventful and we boarded the Italy-bound train there. This took us along the scenic shores of the French Riviera and across the border to Ventimiglia, the first station in Italy. There's a beautiful bike path running through San Remo and going part of the way to Albenga right along the coast. It starts in the small town of Ospedaletti, very close to Ventimiglia, and runs for 24 kilometres terminating at San Lorenzo al Mare where bike riders are forced to re-join the main coastal road. Some years ago the local authorities had the brilliant idea of digging up the railway line which was built on prime real estate and ran adjacent to the coast, as it still does along the French Riviera. Lovely views for train travellers but terrible for those who own property by the tracks with the noise and pollution. The Italians took the train line inland or underground, and have provided a great way for people to travel, under their own steam, along this lovely part of the coast.

ALBENGA

We'd been to Albenga a few weeks previously on our drive back from neighbouring Alassio and not been too impressed. But, as is often the case when staying longer in a place, we really enjoyed our second, longer visit. Staying in a conveniently located bed and breakfast in the old town with its many bars and restaurants gave us many opportunities to explore. Getting our bikes into the storeroom on the first floor of the building was not easy up the steep stairs. But with the owner's assistance we managed and she did not seem overly concerned about the few small scratches we put in the paintwork. We had dinner in a restaurant named *Ricaroka*, not very Italian sounding but the food was definitely so. As is our habit we arrived thirty minutes or so before opening time and even then, as we hadn't booked in advance, were lucky to get the last available table. People streamed in out for takeaways and the place was indeed rocking, or maybe Ricaroking.

The entire region is scattered with beaches and whenever we stopped for a drink there were always many scantily clad natives wandering around. One fellow had found an interesting way of ensuring he was never too far from his phone by inserting in the back of his already too tight swimming trunks. Fortunately it was quite a small phone and I expect he was glad he had not decided to take his iPad to the beach. I also made a mental note to think twice in the future before asking to borrow anyone's phone.

Our route included the port city of Savona which we thought might be a challenge to negotiate. Neither of us was expecting much of Savona but it turned out to be one of the highlights of the trip. The port area is not overly attractive but there was another well-laid bike track running most of the way through town and completely avoiding the port.

We continued our leisurely pace riding along the coast to our destination for the night, the pleasant resort town of Varazze. When we arrived in Varazze and tried to check into our hotel we were greeted, or rather ignored, by a gentleman sunning himself by the front entrance. As we chained our bikes and began removing our luggage, disturbed by the noise we were making, he relocated some-where else. We discovered he was the chef and we later saw him ensconced in front of the television presumably waiting for another shift to start. We had to drop our bags and return at the designated check-in time one hour later even though I'm fairly sure we were the only people staying at the rather run down and out of town establishment. This gave us the opportunity, or rather forced us, to explore the surroundings a little and we were pleased to discover yet another coastal track which would allow us to avoid the hilly main coastal road the next day.

Once checked in we looked forward to taking a refreshing shower but first had to work out how to use the complicated device in the bathroom. The shower in our room looked like something that might once have been rejected by Qaddafi or Ceacescu as being too ostentatious. Various spouts issued from the wall and ceiling while the controls, numerous knobs and dials, resembled the flight deck of a 747 (I've never seen the flight deck of an A380 – they don't allow that sort of thing these days). As we vainly attempted to obtain a flow of water which would not either flood the bathroom, or scald our already slightly sunburned bodies, we wondered who really needs such a complicated device. How we longed for one temperature knob and an on–off button.

TO GENOA AND BEYOND

Most of the way between Varazze and the suburbs of Genoa, there was a good, mainly traffic free, bike track again following an old railway line. We weren't looking forward to traversing Genoa itself but ultimately it turned out to be fairly easy even on a Monday morning. However, as we left the city environs to complete our day's riding, the sky darkened and ominous grey clouds began to appear. Sure enough within minutes the first few drops of rain had begun to fall and only a little later a full blown storm had developed. We struggled on – we really had little choice – there are only so many cappuccino stops one can make in a day, and we vainly hoped the rain would clear. Of course it didn't. In fact it became worse.

Our selected accommodation for the night was situated in a quiet hilltop village. As we rode towards it I really felt we were ascending, as opposed to descending, into hell. Wind squalls exacerbated the effects of the rain and the more we climbed the worse it became. As is so often the case, the nearer we got to our destination the harder it became to find. I had the address, *57 via Chiesa* but did such a number exist? Seemingly not – 55, 56, 58, and then 57a all came into view. Overcoming my usual reticence I accosted a local postman who was, with a wonderful degree of synchronicity, doing his rounds and inquired as to the location of our destination. Unfortunately in my excitement I confused the number 57 with 47 (my Italian was not much improved from over forty years previously) which was in fact the house we were both standing right in front of. He looked at me quizzically before smiling benignly at the poor fool, who had obviously lost at least one of his marbles, and pointing to the house we were standing in front of. We pedalled on before I realized my mistake when we stopped again, the equally drenched postie reappeared. *No, not 47,* I said in my best, worst Italian, *57.* He smiled again and pointed to a well-hidden number painted on the wall opposite.

RAPALLO TO MONTEROSSO CINQUE TERRE BY TRAIN

Another day of riding brought us to the city of Rapallo. Once settled in there we decided on a day off the bikes and went by train to the first village of the Cinque Terre, an area of rugged coastline and five beautiful if somewhat touristy villages. I knew from previous experience that buying tickets at any station where you don't speak the language fluently can be, at best, stressful and at worst, a disaster. In order to avoid this potentially embarrassing and traumatic situation I downloaded the Trenitalia app and went online. We planned a short day so I booked tickets on trains leaving Rapallo at 10:30 with a return at 16:30. Time enough, we figured, for a pleasant stroll around this picturesque region along the coast.

In fact it was more than enough. When we arrived in Monterosso I was amazed at the crowds of tourists alighting from the train. It was only early June, not yet anything near high season, but the hordes descending from the train reminded me of early morning rush hour at Oxford Street Station forty years ago. There were a few differences – everybody was wearing shorts and looked, at least slightly, happy. We shuffled down the stairs towards the exit, an Asian couple, too polite to fight against the tide, waited patiently at the foot of the stairs with their giant suitcases. I imagine they had a long wait. Finally emerging from the melee onto the street below, I was surprised to hear what sounded like Tracy maniacally ringing her bicycle bell. It turned out to be another equally histrionic female, presumably a local late for her shift somewhere, descending a hill at what I considered to be a far from safe pace, irritated by the huge crowds who were, in all likelihood, responsible for her living, blocking her path. Once we had traversed the narrow street and stood gazing at the sea beyond I knew that we had booked a far-too-late-return train. I was ready to leave immediately.

But we'd come this far so at least a stroll along the cliff paths towards the next village had to be done. We wandered around the village itself for a while and then headed off along the precipitous cliff walk. It was pleasant enough and, considering the number of people who had alighted from the train, surprisingly quiet. Rounding a corner we discovered why. Sitting in a small wooden booth was a multilingual ticket seller who requested the sum of 7.50 euros for us to continue along the path. This was reason enough for me to immediately turn around and head back to the station. I figured we could just take an earlier train back to our accommodation and escape this picturesque hell-hole. But no, someone in the *let's make our ticket buying as complicated as we possibly can* department of Trenitalia, the Italian state rail company, had been working overtime. The friendly lady behind the glass screen explained that we could only change our tickets for a later train than the one we had already booked. She then added that, in fact, as we had purchased them online, we could not change them at all. I bit the bullet as the idea of four more hours surrounded by American teens in skimpy tops and German pensioners, almost as revealingly dressed, was simply too much to bear. At great expense I purchased new tickets. We had an enjoyable ride back on a speeding inter-city train, far superior to the regional one we should have been on a few hours later. The train tickets cost about the same as the path access so I felt it was a good trade-off.

GIRL ON A TRAIN

Having successfully, if not financially so, exchanged our tickets we boarded the stylish intercity train headed for Milan and stopping at Rapallo. Comfortably seated we were joined by a young female, slightly outsized by her back pack, who took one of the two seats opposite us. She acknowledged us by smiling lightly in our direction and then proceeded to get set up for what was obviously going to be a long trip. Her first action was to place some sort of internet Bluetooth, time travel, communicator device on the narrow sill of the carriage window and activate it with her secret code. She then took a swig from the water bottle which perfectly matched her day pack. Adequately refreshed she extracted her iPhone, iPad and what I can only guess was some other kind of i-device from the perfectly coordinated pack. She typed a short message of some kind, I assume to whomever had seen her off at the station we had just left, and then proceeded to studiously work on one or another of the larger devices she had with her. I assumed at this stage she held a high ranking role at NASA and was calculating the trajectory of a planned Mars mission, or maybe an as-yet-unpublicised secret mission to one of the outer planets or beyond. I was slightly surprised when she then extracted a notebook of the old fashioned paper variety and began actually writing in it. A little later she attempted, with limited success, to draw a flower of which she had taken a picture on her electronic device. I was impressed by her independence but couldn't help but feel she would have benefitted from the occasional conversation with fellow travellers.

My thoughts drifted back to my own wandering days, many years previously. These consisted of countless seemingly endless train journeys in India before the advent of bottled water when, in order to quench a constant thirst, a highlight was the purchase of *chai* from a station vendor – and the epitome of excitement – hurling the used clay drinking vessel from the train at a sleeping cow. These days, apart from the increased comfort of well-designed backpacks and matching water bottles, it seems the world explorer is never more than a nanosecond or two away from their friends and loved ones. The sad old days of amusing oneself in a Bombay dive hotel by either watching an Indian fashion show on the fuzzy TV or reading a much thumbed Harold Robbins novel are long gone. Equally so, the effort required to painstakingly squeeze as many lines of spidery handwriting as possible onto an aerogramme, always realizing, just as space was at a premium, that you had not added that salient fact which would probably assure you the Nobel Prize for literature. Feelings of envy mixed with nostalgia for a simpler time and lulled by the rhythm of the train I drifted into a reverie of how times had changed.

NOW AND THEN

Most of the time the world around us changes slowly and we hardly notice how things differ from day to day or week to week. There are some exceptions to this rule – the first moon landing and the outbreak of war, or the announcement of peace – but generally, we don't notice how technology, fashion and customs vary from one day to the next before they have completely swamped us.

Musing on the way advances in technology have affected us, I realized that, during the original tandem trip, neither Alan nor I had taken any photos. We didn't have, or even consider buying, a camera. The only photograph I possess to remind me of the fact that the trip happened at all is one donated by the local paper and taken outside Alan's mother's house a day or two before departure. It shows two ridiculously young, well-dressed – too well dressed to be embarking on any kind of adventure – urchins straddling a tandem which actually looks too small for the taller fellow at the back. The lack of photographic equipment to record my adventures persisted for a number of years and it was only due to my brother's insistence, and financial assistance, that I eventually bought a camera, the renowned Olympus Trip 35, a week or so before departing for India. I had imagined myself writing down detailed descriptions of my various adventures and putting them all in a book on my return. As my brother himself had quite recently returned from a trip across Africa in a Land Rover, he knew the value of being able to record what happened for posterity. The trusty Olympus accompanied me on many later trips and endured well, despite being stuffed into bags and dropped on many occasions. These days we all have a camera of one sort or another integrated into our mobile phone. Only the true professional has any need of a separate camera.

The ease of communication is something else which has changed dramatically over the years between the two trips, due of course also to the invention of the mobile phone. Much more than just a phone these days, more a complete communication device superior even to the now antiquated looking gadgets used in *Star Trek*, the modern phone also enables the user to take pictures. This facility is frequently abused. We must all be aware of how many unwanted pictures we receive from our on-line friends. During the original trip the only way I had of communicating with my friends and relatives was by letter. Phone calls were possible but would have involved far more expense and time than we were prepared to invest and were only to be used in an emergency. The concept of *poste restante*, which we used frequently, still exists but is surely, somewhat ironically, used only in emergencies. The excitement of pitching up at the main post office of whichever town or city has been designated as a contact point is not often experienced nowadays. It's been replaced by weekly, daily, sometimes even hourly updates via email, messaging and other information-sharing applications. This may be more efficient but has negated another long forgotten aspect of the post office visit, the possibility, while waiting to collect the often disappointing and mundane news from home, of making a new friend or meeting a new travelling companion.

IN RAPALLO

We were staying at a bed and breakfast place around twenty minutes' walk from the main, tourist-infested town. The owners, Alessandro and Angelo were two of the nicest people we met on the entire trip. Angelo greeted us on arrival and, between immediately extolling the deliciousness of some local fruit which grew in his small garden and explaining, in a very short time, all that we should see in his town, he admired our bikes. He then proceeded to explain in, I thought, far too much detail how much he loved his wife who would be arriving home soon. He had the slightly disconcerting habit of switching, often mid-sentence, between grammatically incorrect but still perfectly coherent English and his mellifluous native language. Obviously for such an impassioned subject as the beauty of the strange bug-like fruit he continually proffered, he needed to employ the one language he felt truly comfortable with.

When his wife returned from work and came to say hello she was indeed very nice but unfortunately did not seem to think she needed to shower or apply deodorant very often, if at all. She also proceeded to embark on a long diatribe about the glories of the local area. Unfortunately her aquaphobia continued as she served us breakfast the next day. I assumed the garrulous Angelo had a very limited sense of smell or was so much in love with his wife, he just did not notice her earthy scent. Of course he may have liked it that way. After all they did have two children.

RAPALLO TO DEIVA MARINA

We left Rapallo still heading east and rode along the coast as far as we could. Due to the cliffs abutting the coastline the road goes inland some way and is quite hilly. With our electric bikes the hills were no real problem and the views were spectacular so we enjoyed being away from the crowds which, as it was approaching high season, were doubtless swarming the coast.

About halfway to our destination we found ourselves back on the coast road. We were faced with a series of tunnels of varying length through the hills. The tunnels operated on a timed, one way system, and were monitored by traffic lights which changed every fifteen minutes. What we didn't realize until we approached the first one was that bikes, even electric ones were not supposed to use them. However as there were two other cyclists admiring the view and waiting for the lights to turn green we assumed the no-bikes rule, like so many other laws in Italy, was a suggestion, not a rule. What we didn't know was that our fellow tunnel riding cyclists were actually French Canadian, not locals, and they had little respect for foreign laws. The lights went green and we pedalled off. As we entered the first, relatively short tunnel, I thought our decision was not so bad. The tunnel was only a few hundred metres long and cars did not seem concerned that we were sharing the space. After a further few hundred metres we began to see the folly of our decision. The next tunnel was over two kilometres long and, as we plunged into its depths, a few people following started hooting and getting more excited than is usual, even for Italians. One fellow in particular, driving a delivery van of some kind which was a bit wider than the various Fiats and other vehicles squeezing past, yelled out of his open window a stream of abuse and invective which I assume was not complimentary. We rode on. We had no choice now as, even if we wanted to turn back and take a longer more difficult route over the hills, we would have had to navigate the tunnels we had already passed through. Hoping there would only be one or two more highways to hell we continued and hoped none of the mainly van-driving delivery oafs were going to stop and show us, in a more physical way, how annoyed they were at our breaking their tunnel use laws. We encountered five more tunnels but fortunately none was quite as long as the previous ones and we lived to tell the tale. If my brain had not tried to black out the memory I would also have learnt some useful Italian phrases of abuse. This was not an experience I would wish to repeat.

Our accommodation in Deiva Marina was a beautiful, if remote, apartment on the ground floor of a large house owned by a lawyer who told us he lived in Genoa during the week and spent most weekends in this charming village. It had been a showery day but once the rain cleared it became a beautiful calm evening. Calm that is, except for the hourly chiming of the village church bell.

The chiming of a bell is quite common in villages like the one we were in. But this particular one had a special feature. It didn't just chime once each hour: it chimed twice.

What foolery is this, I wondered. Fortunately our accommodation was a few hundred metres outside the village, I could only imagine how little sleep those living in houses closer to the building would get. This noise pollution reminded me of the first time we stayed in a guest house near Bangkok in Thailand. We have since become firm friends with the Canadian owner and his Thai wife but the first time we stayed we were amazed to be awoken at five in the morning by a radio broadcast, not from the host himself but broadcast throughout the entire village at high volume. When we staggered down for breakfast at seven he told us it was some kind of weather forecast and grain stock update designed to wake up the farmers. Have these people never heard of alarm clocks? Fortunately when we visited again a few months later the racket was over. Apparently the wires to the cheap distorting speakers had rotted or, more likely in my opinion, been cut and in typical Thai style no one could be bothered to repair them. This was ultimately a good thing as had the noise continued we would probably not have returned to the village and never become firm friends with Chris and his wife Areeya. We've since done some fabulous bike trips with the redoubtable Chris in various parts of Thailand and the surrounding countries of Laos and Vietnam, something that wouldn't have happened had the farmers early morning mandatory wakeup call continued.

DEIVA MARINA TO LEVANTO

Riccardo, our host for the couple of days we spent in Deiva Marina recommended taking the coastal path from the neighbouring village of Framura along the coast to Levanto. The presence of a number of hills between Deiva Marina and the starting point of Framura meant either taking a three minute train ride or a lengthy and undulating bike ride through the hills. We opted for the train, especially as we wanted to familiarise ourselves with the station and the accessibility of Italian trains when travelling with bikes. We'd discovered the station the previous day and knew that the ticket office was only open between the hours of 08:00 and 13:00, so we planned to arrive just after 08:00 to give us time to purchase tickets and quiz the staff about plans for our more complicated return to Ventimiglia the following day. There was a very friendly and helpful fellow on duty and tickets were purchased with no fuss. We heaved our bikes up and down various stairs and waited for the train to arrive to take us to Framura. It was something of a challenge lifting our heavy bikes onto the train but we managed.

On alighting at Framura we assumed finding the bike path would be simple. There were signs everywhere for bike rental, but strangely none for how to access the actual track which we had been told started right from the station. In fact we could see the track tantalizingly close on the other side of the station but no obvious means of access. Eventually the tourist office opened and we were told where to go. On the way we also saw the signs which pointed very clearly to the start of the path. We set off but both felt after our travels so far that the famed path was a little disappointing. Not least because a good 70% of it went through more tunnels and therefore afforded absolutely no views. Access to the starting point was also a little odd. First we went through a short tunnel and down a steep path which took us around a small harbour. There we found an elevator which was just about big enough for one bike and one person. You squeezed into the elevator with your bike and upon exiting found yourself at the start of the bike track. Fortunately it was not yet high season and a weekday, but I can only imagine what kind of queues would form on a busy weekend. Plans for a small bridge, preferably with no steps, from the station across the railway tracks must surely be sitting on someone's desk at the Trenitalia development office.

HEADING HOME TO MANDELIEU
BY TRAIN

Our few days cycling in Italy had come to an end and we were pleased that, apart from one wet day, we had had a pleasant and interesting but uneventful journey. Now and then Tracy's bike had played up, the motor seemed to have a slight fault and did not always provide all the power it should. My own German-made, and therefore surely superior bike continued to click at various times but otherwise performed well.

We packed up our few belongings and headed down the hill from the village where we had been staying to the station for our early morning train. Electric bikes are wonderful for those of us who are not as fit or young (or as stupid) as we would like to be, taking the pain out of steep inclines and allowing the cyclist to enjoy the scenery more. However when it comes to boarding trains their added weight makes things difficult. And then there are the stairs. In this enlightened age many places cater for the disabled by providing ramps and lifts to allow those with limited mobility access to buildings and stations. This facility is also of great help to cyclists. Deiva Marina station did not seem to be one of those places. There was some kind of elevator but it was out of order. And, despite our frantic searching, ramps of any kind could not be found. We soon became adept at sharing the weight of our bikes and carrying them up and down the stairs. At least to complete such an operation in a station there is adequate time.

Boarding a train is not so simple. As soon as each train stopped we would heave our bikes up the steps to enter the train. Then as the train began to move and inevitably sway we had to lift them up at least two more steps into the small open carriage at the rear, or sometimes the front, designated for the carriage of bicycles. This added even more excitement, or stress, to the procedure as, if we were waiting in the wrong place, we would have to quickly mount up and pedal through the mass of other travellers to the correct carriage. Once aboard the fun was not over. Next came the challenge of safely securing the bikes in case of any particularly steep curves which could easily cause a heavily laden bike to topple over. This operation was often made particularly tricky as, due to the hilly terrain, the train would inevitably enter a tunnel just after leaving the station and we would be plunged into darkness. With no visual reference point it is difficult enough to balance, let alone hold on to a bicycle.

CHANGING TRAINS IN GENOA

We relaxed during the short, hour or so journey to Genoa where, according to the helpful fellow who had sold me the train tickets a couple of days previously, there would be a 40 minute connection for another train to Ventimiglia and the border with France. On arrival in Genoa we searched in vain for the platform for our next train. On consulting the timetable I spotted the ominous phrase *festivi e sabato (festivals and Saturdays)*. We were travelling on a Saturday so our connecting train did not operate. This explained why, when I had tried to check it earlier on the Trenitalia website, I had been unable to find it.

No matter, there was another train at 11:43 so we relaxed in Genoa and took a walk around wondering why there were so many Australian tourists in town. As the time approached for our departure we headed for the platform and while we waited, hoping we were at the correct end of the train, were befriended by a local who was also taking his bike on the train to France and intending to cycle from

Nice to the rather vague destination of 'The Pyrenees'. When the train arrived he helped us board, bemoaning the state of his nation's train system as being from the 19th Century. We never learned his name but he took great care in ensuring, when two ruffians boarded the train, beer bottles in hand, to protect his bike and ours by standing in the vestibule and keeping an eye on them. I tried to have a conversation with our guardian as he spoke quite good English but it wasn't easy over the loud music that the oiks were playing on their phones while they imbibed and smoked. At one stage our new found friend became quite annoyed and shouted something, presumably not complimentary, at the two scallywags who responded with a sneer. But they were just teenagers doing what teenagers do and meant no harm. In fact they reminded me of myself and my teenage pals fifty or so years previously who, although we had no means of playing music on trains, were certainly up for boozing and smoking where we shouldn't.

As we got to know the guy a little more we realized he was something of an angry fellow. Retired some years previously from teaching science at a local school, a job he seemed to have hated, he confided in us that he had recently left his wife, *always complains*, he said and decided to travel the world, mainly Europe so far, on his bike. He had a good heart that's for sure as evidenced by his ceaseless desire to assist us with our heavy bikes and his role as self-appointed guardian of all things bicycle related. But I couldn't help but think he was a lonely, slightly bitter character. Perhaps once he reached The Pyrenees his mood would improve. We saw him again briefly at the station in Ventimiglia. There was some timetable confusion due to the continuing French rail strikes. Our Italian friend was headed for Nice and we helped him board the train waiting on the platform but before we could board ourselves the doors closed and it departed. We never saw him again.

TANDEM MEMORIES

Over the few weeks before we had embarked on our Italian trip my bike developed an annoying clicking sound. It emanated from the back wheel somewhere. I had nearly fallen off many times trying see exactly where it was coming from while riding along, all to no avail. After tightening and lubricating everything that could be tightened and lubricated I had the bike checked by a mechanic. Twice, at different workshops. No luck. During the trip the noise worsened and I was sure that at some stage something was going to give. It survived though and I knew that I would have to either live with it for the next few months or contact someone in Germany to fix it. In my continuing efforts for a solution and, as is often the way with minor ailments, I took the bike to a third specialist in hope of him finding the reason for the noise. Yet again, after fiddling with the gears for a while, applying grease, oil and some other undefined lubricants he declared the issue fixed. I was doubtful but I dropped ten euros in his tip jar and pedalled off. As expected after about five minutes the noise returned, as bad as ever. I considered returning to the shop but it was hot, traffic was bad and I knew it would be futile. As with the trusty tandem years previously I just decided to live with it until it became impossible to ride further. On the original trip, due to a lack of tools and skill, we had little choice but to just carry on regardless unless a problem made the bike completely unrideable, which, much to my frequent disap-pointment, it never did.

GENOA AGAIN

Coincidentally, a week after the trip to Italy I went back to Genoa again for a work conference. This time I travelled in style by air conditioned bus and stayed in a four star hotel situated near the attractive harbour. As is invariably the way with such events the conference itself was quite dull but I met some nice people.

I sat through countless hours of presentations, stifling yawns and convinced that I had seen all of the endless slides being shown before, many times. I forced myself to stay partially conscious, but one afternoon, just after lunch, was unable to avoid drifting into a reverie where I imagined myself being immortal.

He caught my eye as I stepped off the bus from Delhi. Amidst the cries of 'Sir, Sir,' his stood out for some reason. His appearance was not greatly different from the many other people milling around the bus: other passengers simply looking for the relatives who were due to meet them; some looking for a taxi; the majority looking for an unsuspecting tourist (we hated being called that, we were travellers) on which to pounce in an attempt to sell some piece of useless junk.

But I'd been in India for a couple of months and I knew how to avoid such scams. Or so I thought. Keeping my head high I marched imperiously away from the bus as if to some prearranged destination. And I kept walking. Away from the melee at the bus stand, through the bazaar and on towards the small group of teashops which lined the adjacent street. I did not look back or change my pace. I selected the least filthy looking of the shops and took a seat at a rickety table. 'Chai', I said loudly to the boy who was lazily swatting flies with a dirty rag.

As I breathed in the sweet sticky air and relished the relative quiet the fellow from the bus stand appeared again. 'Sir,' he said almost pleadingly, 'you must listen to me. I have a gift for you. Take this potion and you will live forever.' To this day I have no idea why I followed his instructions. Drinking an unknown substance proffered by a scruffy stranger in India is simply asking for trouble. But for some reason I obliged his request.

Having swallowed the liquid I looked around expecting to now be asked for a sum of money, but the unwelcome local had vanished as quickly as he had appeared. I checked my bag. My money and passport were untouched.

I thought little more of the incident as I continued with my six month trip.

It was only after I arrived home and began telling people about my experiences on the sub-continent that it occurred to me something strange had taken place. Everyone kept asking, 'But surely you got sick. Everyone who goes to India gets sick.' It's true that in the first couple of months of my travels I had spent a few uncomfortable nights hunched over a foul smelling Indian latrine wishing I were somewhere else. But in the latter stages of my journey I had had no problems. I had put it down to luck, frequent hand washing and acclimatisation. But the more I thought about it the more I realized I had had no illness whatsoever since my chance meeting in the Pondicherry market with the squint-eyed charlatan. No headaches, no toothache, no stomach troubles. Nothing.

That was 30 million years ago. Now I drift in space. The need for a corporeal entity has long since passed. Only my spirit has survived. Every millennia or so the solar winds take me to a place where I can communicate with others like myself. But mostly I am destined to drift for all eternity, alone.

As you can imagine, a lot has happened in those years. The human race didn't destroy the planet or annihilate itself. Disease and hunger were finally eradicated. I eventually moved back to France.

From a scientific perspective various prophecies came true, although not precisely at the time it was thought they would. It took man much longer than expected to safely reach Mars or any other part of the solar system. Venturing further required a lot of time but was eventually achieved. I won't bore you with details of the science required. Did we ever contact aliens? Of course, and they were very helpful. How else do you think man left the solar system?

Many mysteries of life still remain unsolved. These include such things as: Why people think tattoos are attractive in any way. Why dancing is considered fun. Why anyone likes rap or electronic music. What is exciting about watching sport? Why children always shout. Why fat guys wear T-shirts. It's a long list. I could go on for ever (I really could).

On a more personal level, in the first hundred years or so I amused myself by learning every known language and travelling wherever I pleased. Mainly I travelled and studied because, once my family and friends had all died, I found it harder to socialise. People's mundane experiences interested me less and less – they had never interested me much – and how was I supposed to contribute to the conversation? *A hundred and twenty years ago I went to India and...*, who would believe me? More importantly who would care? I suppose I became a bit of a bore because I really did know everything. Sometimes it was fun to sit and listen to people's ramblings but mostly even that tired me.

I took on various jobs every decade or so to experience them for myself. It helped, in a small way, to pass the time. I wasn't in it for the money, I was never in it for the money, but earning a salary became futile around 200 years after my return from India. The end to war ensured that Earth's bountiful resources could finally be used to fulfil people's needs and wants whatever they might be.

Religion slowly died out as people realized, especially after the first alien contact was made, that God may have once existed but he certainly didn't anymore. It was, as any right minded person knows, the abuse of religious belief that had caused most of the wars on Earth, so once it was finally accepted that all those beliefs were based on unsubstantiated falsehoods and misinterpreted stories handed down over generations, there was no longer any need to fight about it. There was nothing to prove.

With war eradicated, resources could also be used to improve agricultural growth and feed Earth's burgeoning population. Communications continued to improve and the invention of the matter transporter around the year 3200 allowed people to move freely with minimal effort.

But nothing lasts forever, except me. Life on my home planet survived for a few thousand years – it was an interesting experience detachedly watching man's advances in science, arts and philosophy.

The human race died out eventually of course. We evolved over time into a mix of human and biomedical machines. But humankind as a whole was unable to make the leap to the purely spiritual level. I, on the other hand, had no choice.

Sometimes I envy them their mortality. I've had a lot of time to think about it.

There is a certain part of all of us that lives outside of time. Perhaps we become aware of our age only at exceptional moments and most of the time we are ageless. (Milan Kundera)

A loud sneeze from one of my colleagues interrupted my reverie. It was finally time for a break and we all gratefully stood up, yawned, stretched and headed out into the foyer.

The food was good at least, and the cappuccinos, most of which came with some kind of custard filled donuts, delicious.

Genoa has its attractions but they do not reveal themselves immediately. This may be why Christopher Columbus decided not to stay home. In the little spare time I had, I wandered the streets near the hotel taking photographs and avoiding the advances, as best I could, of the African immigrants who occupied every corner. They were simply trying to eke out a living selling various trinkets but their large numbers did make them a little intimidating. I managed to circumvent any difficult situations and ended up in a somewhat atmosphere-less bar. It purported to be an Irish bar but the name of *The Britannia* threw a slight amount of ethnic confusion into the mix. I had a slightly flat pint of Kilkenny (normally one of my favourite beers) with my buddy Ray, who spent most of the time referring to one or the other of his two phones. We finished our pints and returned to the hotel deciding to leave any further exploration of Columbus' home town for another day.

ENFIELD TO HERNE BAY – 2018

They say the road to hell is paved with good intentions. This aphorism can also be applied to my rerun bike trip. In the end even the short two days from Enfield, where it all began, to Herne Bay didn't happen. I had certainly intended to make my way into London and take the train again from Liverpool Street where I had first met the redoubtable Alan, out to the north London suburb of Enfield and from there to ride through east London to Tilbury where I would take the ferry across the Thames to Gravesend, stay the night in a cosy guest house and ride on to Herne Bay the next day. But as I studied the map and details of what was involved I decided it would be so much easier and more pleasant to simply ride from Crowborough in Sussex, where I was planning to collect another of my late brother's stored bikes, this time a standard non-electric one and then ride from there direct to Herne Bay. It would even be possible in one day but I intended to take two. This decision simply proved another aphorism – you can never really go back.

There's a school of scientific thought that says when

time travel is invented, as it will surely one day be, it will still only be possible to travel back in time from a time after the invention, to another time still after the invention. Meaning it won't be possible to travel back to any chosen point in time, say to the time of Jesus and witness the crucifixion, or to Hitler's early days and remove him from history in some way. In reality this truism exists now. We can travel back physically to a place from our past, but we can never re-live the time we were there. This restriction may or not be technically true as we are nowhere near inventing time travel. During the not infrequent spells of utter boredom I have experienced at work, I spent lengthy periods considering the possibility of travelling through time, in any direction. If only to travel forward by a few hours and end another desk bound day. The possibilities intrigued me so much that I wrote two stories centred on the subject. I based my fantasy on my three favourite subjects: the TV show *Star Trek*, the music of Bruce Springsteen and the writings of Henry Miller. They have little or nothing to do with cycling but they surely deserve a place in this book.

BRUCE, HENRY AND TIME MANAGER – PART 1

The year was 2365

Picard was not happy. 'What happened, Mr O'Brien? Why do I have two cultural icons of the 20th century in my transporter bay?'

'I'm not sure Captain. A malfunction in the Heisenberg compensators. I'll fix it immediately.'

'Make it so,' commanded Picard as he strode away.

Worf groaned, 'Security to the transporter bay. A straggle haired singer and a balding writer have been erroneously beamed aboard the Enterprise. They may be dangerous. Take all necessary precautions.'

O'Brien was quick to rectify his mistake. Too quick perhaps. He adjusted the targeting scanners and sent the two unexpected visitors back to their respective time periods. Or so he thought.

He was certainly successful in removing the two reluctant intruders from the Enterprise but, unknown to him, he was not so successful in calculating the correct destinations for either of them. In his haste not to incur Picard's wrath he had accidentally pressed the recently installed 2-4-1 button and, instead of dispatching the unwitting inter-lopers to their original time periods, had sent them both to southern France, Earth circa 2015.

'Humans are a strange looking race,' muttered Worf as he continued with his daily task of maintaining a safe ship, unaffected by writers and rock stars, not that he really had any idea what either of these things were.

Those two cultural icons were Henry Miller and Bruce Springsteen.

Well known now to anyone with even a passing interest in literature or music, success had not come overnight for either of them.

While he did achieve some level of notoriety later in life, Henry really only became famous, some might say infamous, posthumously. For the first 33 years of his life he lived a hand to mouth existence, well documented in many of his books but perhaps never better than in *Plexus*, the second volume of quasi memoir *The Rosy Crucifixion*.

Bruce's first two albums had not sold well. His recording contract was under review as he worked on what would become his breakthrough album, *Born to Run*.

The year was 1939

Henry had found a publisher for his first book *Tropic of Cancer* but apart from his various benefactors and cronies as he would have called them, nobody had taken much inter-est. His second novel *Black Spring* had suffered the same ignominious fate. He was thinking that it was maybe time to give up the struggle. He knew that, once you have given up the ghost, everything follows with dead certainty, even in the midst of chaos. Henry was, as ever, also thinking about sex.

The year was 1975

Bruce had been walking along 57th Street where he had narrowly avoided being involved in an incident. It was a hot New York day and he'd taken the bus most of the way into town. As always he'd told the bus driver to keep the change and given him some other useful advice. He was headed for the recording studio. In his head the words and musical structure of such future classics as *Backstreets* and *Jungleland* were taking shape. He had another song running around his head which he knew he could make it big with. He was planning to call it *Born to Run*. Bruce was, as ever, also thinking about Sax.

Such were the mind-sets of Bruce and Henry when, still deep in their individual thoughts, they heard a strange tinkling sound.

'Maybe I could use that in a song,' thought Bruce.

'Is that a ghost?' thought Henry.

When the sound stopped they were standing on curious-looking silver plates in what appeared to be some kind of hospital operating theatre. A curly haired Irishman stood behind a console looking confused. A shaven headed man in a red uniform entered the room.

'Handsome guy,' thought Henry.

Before either Bruce or Henry had time for further thought they heard the sound once more and found themselves transported again.

This time their corporeal entities reappeared in a small French hilltop village near the city of Nice on the Cote d'Azur.

Henry was the happiest man alive. He'd long dreamed of visiting Europe, France particularly, and now here he was in Nice, France. Sure, it all looked different from what he'd seen in the picture books but people were speaking French and he was more than content.

'Where are all the broads?' he muttered salaciously.

Bruce giggled and said 'It's too bright here, I'm blinded by the light.' He jumped up, turned around, spit in the air, fell on the ground and asked which was the way back home. All the while thinking to himself, 'Why didn't the bus stop at 82nd Street?'

As they stood at the side of the road Andrew, a friendly company employee, used to helping out bewildered looking foreigners, stopped and inquired how he could be of assistance.

They clambered aboard what Henry referred to as a *jalopy* and Bruce as *nice wheels*, both marvelling at the switches and dials in the modern looking vehicle. As they drove along the winding roads and through the hills they gave an account, as best they could, of what had befallen them so far that day.

Even though their story sounded implausible in the extreme Andrew did not completely disbelieve them. After all he had conducted training on many of the company's products so he was used to hearing such outlandish tales.

As they searched for a spacc in the vastness of the company car park, and Andrew discovered more about Bruce and Henry's plight, he began to formulate a plan as to how he could help them return to their previous lives.

A day or two later Bruce and Henry sat in the executive briefing centre guzzling the free coffee.

'Man, that TV is huge, I bet it receives at least 57 channels,' thought Bruce.

Henry was enjoying himself eyeing up the sleek-suited ladies who scurried about purposefully.

A young, slim fellow with a slight Australian accent was talking, 'Our plan is to transport you back to your correct time period using one of our new products. We've been developing it secretly for almost 20 years now, ever since our competitors came up with the idea of a Credit Card Payment Gateway.'

Bruce and Henry came from simpler times. Most of what *the suit*, as they had both taken to calling pretty much everyone they had met, was saying went way over their heads but they were both sure that, fascinating as life was in the south of France in 2015, they would rather be back in familiar surroundings. For one thing all the new words and phrases such as granularity, bifurcation, strategic importance, strong customer focus, and something called *big rocks*, were confusing the heck out them.

'Man,' thought Henry, 'these guys are more full of it than me.'

Bruce was rapidly realizing that the lyrics on his first two albums were overly convoluted and vowed to pare things down for his next record.

'I'll go for the Samurai approach,' he thought to himself.

The next day, following a substantial breakfast of not one but two croissants each in the company staff restaurant, Bruce, Henry and around 25 company staff stood together in the Aconcagua meeting room. The excitement was palpable. A mixture of languages – French, Spanish, Hindi, even some English – merged together in a creative cacophony.

The new company product *Time Manager* wasn't quite working at 100% efficiency yet. Training had started a while ago of course but there was still some fairly major functionality missing and the reporting module was a mess. However, early adoption is vital and there was an important business case for this new product release to succeed. What a dull place the world would be without the rest of Bruce's albums or Henry's books.

After a short speech, mainly focussing on how he was

confident there would be increased functionality in future releases, the newly appointed Director of Time, recently relocated from Bangkok to Nice, pressed the enter key. Bruce and Henry glittered slightly in the morning sunlight and disappeared.

To be continued…

BRUCE, HENRY AND TIME MANAGER – PART 2

The year was 2308

LA Island had been created by the massive San Andreas quake of 2105. It was now home to most of Earth's high-tech corporations which had relocated there when Silicon Valley became a vast inland sea. I'd beamed into the BransonMusk Headquarters some years previously from the lake resorts of Central Australia.

My transportation had been one of the first – I always was an early adopter and outlier. Flying was an option but I'd decided against 24 hours cooped up in a cramped space breathing other people's waste gases and trying to sleep while being buffeted, not by bad weather but the alien passenger behind me using my seatback as an aid to lift his gravity challenged body. And I really could not watch another episode of *Modern Family* on a tiny TV screen. The new hyper drive craft could shave a few hours off the journey time but there were still all the check-in and security procedures to endure.

These days *travel by wire*, as it was originally called, is commonplace. Sure there have been a few mishaps.

Protons dissipating into space. Partially successful beam-outs resulting in a once-healthy, happy human arriving at his destination as a soup of disconnected atoms. A few unlucky travellers had even lost their molecules.

Statistically though, matter transport remains safer than hypersonic, supersonic or subsonic flight has ever been. The Gravity Drive Subterranean Train marketing slogan, *42 minutes from anywhere to anywhere else*, was still in its infancy. A technical overview of the GDST (branding are still working on the product name) can be found at the following internet coordinates:

http://www.physicscentral.com/explore/poster-earth.cfm

Recognized by my superiors as an innovator who enjoyed a challenge I had for some years been working on a project to develop a time travel portal. This was an as-yet untapped area of the travel sector and senior management saw great potential.

Later in my distinguished career, to replace a colleague who had been promoted off world, I had willingly agreed to relocate to the space station of Bangkok 123 where the local developers had achieved some interesting results in the area of temporal distortion. These results were mainly due to the appearance of a wormhole they had called Nana Soi 4. The possibilities needed to be further investigated. The move suited me from a personal aspect as well, as my life partner had also recently obtained the position of Counsellor on the same station.

My main objective had been to manage the stable expansion of the wormhole. Wormholes are notorious for their instability, often appearing and disappearing in a wildly fluctuating, unpredictable length of time. They might exist for a matter of seconds, minutes, months or years. This was often related to a phenomenon known as partner rupture, frequently a result of sensors, disrupted by badly calculated alcohol content, giving false readings of gravitational attraction. This would in turn result in previously cohesive, closely bound partner atoms suddenly being split apart with disastrous consequences. This event, which happened all too frequently, was commonly referred to as *disforce*.

Investigating such an anomaly during an away mission with my security advisor Khun Dom on the pleasure planet Soi Cowboy, I had been caught in a rift of the space–time continuum. My assignment, originally planned to be five years, had run on indefinitely.

My increasing desperation to return to my home base was leading me to try more and more outlandish approaches such as:

1. Applying for roles which seemed perfectly suited to my skills and background but inexplicably turned amorphic, shimmering and transforming themselves into positions for which my vast and varied experience was thought invalid. Often it seemed that these roles were only deemed suitable to a specific type of less developed life form than myself.

2. I'd tried thinking out of the box, proposing many bold new approaches to the neural pathways of my superiors, including my Director, Jean-Louis Picard, suggesting original ideas and ways to achieve my aim. Unfortunately they always seemed to be delayed by issues with Starfleet Headquarters.

3. In my free time I'd used my personal holodeck privileges, tirelessly creating scenarios and

fleshing them out with different procedures and schemes to achieve a positive outcome. Only to discover that whatever I did the safety protocols would always cut in and stop my activity before any conclusion could be reached.

My thoughts on the above were interrupted by a loud wailing noise. The emergency klaxon had sounded and I rushed to my station. 'There's been an unauthorised time extraction,' my assistant was saying. 'Two humans from the 20th century have appeared on a Starship called the Enterprise. Downtime consequences could be disastrous. This is a severity 1 urgent.'

Accidental transports from the past were something we had always feared and made every effort to avoid by instigating strict security codes. I quickly took the vacuum elevator to the 900th level where my boss had his office.

Director Picard was talking as I entered the room. 'We need to fix this immediately if not sooner. We're going to send you back to a time some months before the erroneous transport. You'll need to surreptitiously aid the local people in developing the time transporter for this company and use it to relocate these characters to their original time coordinates.'

'Do you have any more details about them?' I asked.

'Only their names, apparently they are called Bruce Springsteen and Henry Miller. Our records show that they changed the face of popular culture immensely and without them the 20th and 21st centuries would have been indescribably dull. In fact the human spirit would have been robbed of much of its creative force. This issue threatens the future of mankind itself.'

As my boss waxed eloquent about the qualities of these two humble men I shuddered slightly, realizing the enormity of the task I had been assigned. I knew we weren't anywhere near ready to accomplish such a complex series of transfers. Sending me back through time and space to somewhere called Biot, France was relatively straightforward. But for me to correctly calculate the co-ordinates to then send this Bruce guy back to 1975 and his pal Henry to 1939 would require all my skills and experience.

I also knew that for me it would probably be a one way trip. The power reserves required to subsequently return me to the 24th century simply did not exist in the 21st century.

To aid concentration I quietly repeated to myself the 3 Step Guide to creating a time machine:

1. Locate a black hole.
2. Calculate the exact location of the event horizon.
3. Create a wormhole by curving space–time.

This was often known by its acronym, LCC.

Sure, I could take all the technology with me and assemble it on arrival but how would I use it without the almost limitless power resources that exist in the 24th century? Earth was by now a type 2 civilisation on the Kardashev scale i.e. one that has harnessed all the power of the sun.

The task would be similar to trying to drive a car in the 18th century. It would only run until the petrol tank was empty. Then how would you fill it up? And it would take an awful lot of candles to power an iPhone.

These were my concerns as I worked on my strategic plan.

Culturally, at least, I was well prepared. Like all members of the TDT (Time Development Team), I had been well trained in the required protocols. I was confident I would be able to fit in without too much trouble, apart perhaps from the odd fashion faux pas.

I had also signed the NDA (Non-Divulgence Agreement). This stipulated that I would keep a low profile and not disclose anything about life in my own time. Basically it meant just keeping my mouth shut while everyone else talked. I saw no problem with that. Maintaining a stoic silence when those around me are spouting utter nonsense was something I had always been good at. Likewise, having my own ideas ignored at the time of utterance only for them to be quoted to me later as original thought was something I handled well.

Part of my mission preparation was to educate myself on the contribution my two charges had made to humankind. As I studied their early artistic output it became clear to me how relevant the ideas promulgated by these two individuals still remained, hundreds of years later. I was allowed by intergalactic law to take a few non-scientific items with me. Naturally I took a memory nanochip of Bruce's first two albums, *Greetings from Asbury Park* and *The Wild, The Innocent...* as it is commonly known. Additionally I knew that a copy of my favourite Henry Miller book, *Plexus* was bound to come in handy. I carried these stored, electronically, in one of my few remaining hair follicles.

I was ready for transport. Ready to shape the future from the past with time travel.

THE ZOCO EFFECT

The *right place right time* anomaly exists in other areas of life as well. There's something I like to call the Zoco effect. Once when travelling in Spain with my good friend Erik we sampled a bottle of the local liqueur called Zoco. Absolutely delicious I thought. We were travelling by car so I bought four bottles of the stuff and transported it back to France intending to impress my friends with this elixir of the gods. One evening after dinner I offered it around to some unsuspecting guests expecting nothing but praise for my excellent find. Everybody, including me, found it disgusting. I spent months after that trying to get rid of it. I tried mixing it with everything, serving it extra cold in an attempt to mask the bitter taste. In the end I found the only way it was even vaguely palatable was when poured over ice cream. The Zoco effect.

SIDE TRIP TO CANTERBURY

During the few days we had in Kent I decided it would be fun to revisit another of my childhood haunts, the school where I had pretty much wasted six years of my life. Canterbury Technical High School for Boys it had been called when, through an unfortunate quirk of fate, I had been selected to attend it. A few years later some pretentious fellow renamed it The Geoffrey Chaucer. This had no noticeable effect on my education. It was bad timing in the extreme that, due to there being a new school built the year after I had taken my 11 plus, there were many of us poor unfortunates for whom it was decided, at the age of eleven, how our education, indeed the rest of our lives, would be conducted. The English education system failed me by deciding, at that tender age, I was best suited to attend a technical school where I was supposed to learn such practical things as woodwork, metalwork and technical drawing. I failed gloriously at all three.

Or did I?

I made a footstool which my Mother used till the day she died, when she occasionally had the chance to rest.

By accidentally picking up a piece of hot metal without protective gloves I attained the distinction, after the excruciating pain had subsided, of being the only boy in school, for a period of some weeks at least, who had no fingerprints on his right hand. The other kids were impressed. I was obviously not to be trifled with.

I learnt how to draw a symmetric five-pointed star. I can't really think of any practical use for that, apart from maybe a career as a sherriff's badge maker, but it makes doodling more fun.

I learnt three things in school: there was more than one Napoleonic war, the St Lawrence Seaway is the longest man-made channel in the world (or at least it was in 1969) and probably most importantly, how to masturbate quietly. Only one of these items has remained useful in later life.

Like many kids, before social norms meant that parents drove their children everywhere, my daily school commute was by bus. How clearly I remember the innumerable times, in all weathers, I took the number 6 from The Queen's Hotel to Canterbury bus station and then hiked another two miles to the Geoffrey Chaucer School for Boys. How I wish I could forget them. In retrospect however, I probably learnt more from the journey than from the endless hours in various badly ventilated classrooms. The educational activities we engaged in during our thirty minute bus trip included discussing the previous night's TV shows such as *Monty Python* and *Top of the Pops*, making fun of each other's latest outrageous addition to the school uniform, and, as these were the days when smoking on buses was still allowed, setting fire to girls' hair. Thermodynamics.

My adventurous spirit developed early, if nothing else

did, and one morning I arranged to make the journey by bike with a couple of schoolboy chums. It's a nine mile trip but back then to us it seemed like we were setting off across the Sahara Desert or planning an ascent of Everest. Not that we planned anything. All I can remember is some vague agreement to meet at 07:30 presumably at some local well-known place in Herne Bay, mutually convenient to our own locales. And we were away. We would only have attempted such an adventure during the brief and often intemperate English summer so I can only imagine how we must have reeked when we dumped our bikes somewhere in the school grounds and, without even thinking about showering or changing our clothes, swaggered in to our first class. Maybe it was biology?

WHITSTABLE TO RECULVER – 2018

As the Scottish poet Robert Burns wrote *The best laid plans of mice and men often go awry.* Although my wife and I had great plans for covering various sections of the original trip together, these continued to be whittled away as time went on. I had long since abandoned any plans to ride from Enfield to Herne Bay and once we reached the small Sussex town of Crowborough, where my brother had lived for the last few years of his life, I was fairly certain the planned ride from there was not like likely to happen either. I'd been to Crowborough before, once just after my brother had purchased a house there and once just after he died. Having explored its limited attractions on foot, I knew it was a hilly area but I did not appreciate quite how hilly until I tried to ride a bike around the local streets. Somewhat spoilt of course by having become used to the assistance an electric bike gives on undulating terrain, I struggled even to ride to the local bike shop where the bikes, which had languished for years in my brother's garage, needed to be serviced. Once informed that the bikes required around 80 pounds each of repairs to make them roadworthy it was an easy decision to abandon the idea of a ride cross country to north Kent. Fortunately some non-refundable overnight accommodation I had booked was also cancelled by the provider and I took this display of providence as a sign that the ride was not to be.

The next day, in heavy rain, we drove to Enfield in north London and took some pictures of the house where Alan and I had started our journey south all those years previously. Nothing much had changed apart from the number of parked cars which now lined the surrounding streets. It was a shame in a way not to be cycling as the borough of Enfield had more cycle paths than I had seen for quite some time in an urban setting. It continued to rain as we explored a little before driving home and, although this reminded me of the inclement weather Alan and I had experienced on our original ride, I was glad not to be struggling through it again.

I could not help but feel that, having come all the way to England to re-live the cycling trip, at least some cycling should be completed. We drove to Herne Bay, the finishing point of the first day's ride in 1976, and rented a couple of bikes in Herne Bay's neighbouring town of Whitstable. The Oyster Bay Trail had recently been constructed along the beachfront. This takes the avid cyclist or walker through the dubious attractions of Whitstable's harbour and out along a concrete track by the beach towards Herne Bay. From there the trail continues along the rugged and windswept north Kent coast through Herne Bay itself, and all the way to the famed Reculver Towers. It then changes to the Viking Coastal Trail and continues on through the towns of Margate, Broadstairs and Ramsgate. Apart from the Towers there's not much at Reculver, but the ride there gave me time to reminisce on the adventures of my misspent youth – are there any other kind? As a child, Reculver had always seemed like the end of the world to me. The Towers were prominent and could easily be seen from anywhere along the coast. Wandering the streets of my little town in my early teens and striding Wordsworth-like along the sea-front, I would gaze longingly at those imposing relics of Roman invasion and dream of a future beyond the confines of my small world.

IAN ROBERT STANLEY 11/07/1950 – 30/01/2015

My brother Ian and I were never very close. Growing up I was the annoying little brother who borrowed, and often broke, his toys. I recall one particular favourite toy train which, in a fit of pique over some long forgotten incident I hurled forcefully – as forcefully as a five year old could – at the wall and watched gleefully as it smashed to a thousand pieces. I remember also once accidentally destroying his portable cassette player and attempting to escape a thumping by riding off with utmost haste on my bicycle.

We had very little in common; he was practical and had a very technical and scientific mind. He could fit kitchens, repair cars and successfully carry out any number of other do-it-yourself tasks. In this he took after my father and this similarity led to no end of *I wouldn't do it like that* arguments.

He was generous. I can't count the number of times I returned to England after one or another failed attempt at living overseas to share whichever house he had recently bought in various London suburbs. I never paid rent and as long as I didn't break anything he always had space for me. He wasn't easy to live with though. Because he was something of a perfectionist, I would always be sure not to leave an odd sock in the washing machine, or to forget to remove the receipt from a shopping bag, before carefully putting it in the cupboard reserved specifically for that purpose.

ONE OF MANY ENDINGS

Whenever a major event is planned it always seems that the months preceding it drag on forever and then finally within a few weeks of the event, suddenly it's there staring you in the face. So it was with our departure from France. We put our flat in Mandelieu on the market and began the process of trying to offload various unwanted items. As we were returning to Australia where we already owned not one, but two, fully furnished apartments we needed nothing from France. We also had bikes in Australia so reluctantly sold our electric bikes – they could only be shipped at great expense and with difficulty.

One of the most poignant acts of our departure was saying goodbye to my collection of ties. Hardly worn these days except for formal occasions such as weddings and funerals, during my illustrious career the tie, or neck-tie as the Americans call it, presumably less there be some confusion as to where on the body it should be worn, had been an important part of any young man's wardrobe. I no longer possessed the fabled yellow knit tie I had worn to my interview with the finance company a few months before departing on my bike trip with Alan, but I did have a number of other stylish examples. Fortunately I had a friend who eschewed modern trends and still, even on casual Fridays, sported one of his many examples of trendy neckwear. In summer he often crossed one of the well-known lines of fashion and would wear a tie with a short sleeved shirt, really not acceptable. He didn't really want my slightly bedraggled collection but I gave it to him anyway.

We also sold, or gave away, as many of our other possessions as we could. One of the items which proved almost impossible to sell was my collection of over a thousand CDs and a fine selection of hi-fi equipment, purchased over a period of more than thirty years. It had become outmoded technology for the most part, but still held many happy memories for me. I tried taking the CDs to a local exchange store where I stood helplessly by as a feckless youth rifled through them, selecting about one in four for the store's purchase. He deemed only about eighty of the shiny discs resalable. This from a total of three hundred, and I received the princely sum of fifty cents for each one.

To avoid experiencing this indignity again I tried offering them free with the sale of a couple of excellent CD players I had purchased during the medium's boom. Well-known models which had cost me the better part of a thousand euros each at the time, much to my wife's annoyance – *How many black boxes do you need?* I offered these for sale at twenty-five euros each, a mere pittance, and threw in the CDs as an added enticement to buy. This brought forth better results, along with a tear to my eye as I watched a very happy French guy pile everything into his open top Peugeot and drive away.

Some items remained and I was eventually forced to give them to a charity organisation. I like to think that occasionally some lucky person, unaffected by the ubiquity of streaming or other services, will one day discover, as I did, a new artist or CD he (or perhaps she) has been looking for and his (or perhaps her) life will be changed in a positive way as they begin their journey down their musical path to Nirvana (the place, not the band).

We had a similar problem with books. Over the years we had amassed a large library of novels, guide books, language books (many of which were virtually untouched), dictionaries and, belonging to my wife, many business related books. Nobody wanted them, certainly nobody wanted to buy them. Local bookshops weren't interested. Everybody has a Kindle these days. Even that is considered old fashioned, so I should say some kind of Kindle-style application. Friends were happy to cherry pick certain items but we were forced to consider the almost sacrilegious act of simply taking them to the local tip. *At least the paper will be re-used* said my wife. One morning, out walking, I discovered, just a few streets away, a small box installed by the local council specifically for swapping books. You left a few there for other locals to peruse and take, and took whatever you wanted. Slowly but surely we redistributed our literary collection among the unsuspecting citizens of Mandelieu. I even invented a phrase to describe the activity – *leaving France five books at a time.*

Each day as I randomly selected a few books to dispatch I would be pleasantly, if somewhat egotistically, reminded of my eclectic reading tastes. This culminated one late July morning as, purely by chance I selected a couple to recycle – Rod Stewart's hilarious autobiography, inventively called *Rod* and Solzhenitsyn's equally factual but more depressing *One Day in the Life of Ivan Denisovich*. I imagined some Anglophile French person struggling over the decision of which to take. As we watched our book collection slowly diminish I became quite nostalgic. We all have a strange attachment to books. Perhaps not so much to the actual content but to the memories attached to the purchase and reading of them. Many of the numerous paperbacks I had consumed over the years were now spotted brown with age and smelt musty from long periods of storage in humid or damp conditions. I wasted much time when I should have been more productively engaged with other things, such as writing this book, picking up one or another of my previous purchases and, intending to only read the back cover, found myself sitting down and beginning the book over again. Unfortunately, unlike CDs, it's not possible, certainly not in any practical way, to scan each book onto a device and save it electronically.

As I time wasted and pondered I travelled back in my head to my days on the number 6 bus to work in Canterbury where, as a slightly pretentious twenty year old, I had read, and tried to understand the works of Nietzsche and Jean Paul Sartre – Sartre's first novel *Nausea* was the first real book I ever read – while others were devouring what I considered to be simple fayre such as Tolkien. I also reminisced on the many hours spent commuting to London where, between naps, I would studiously attempt to plough through the great Russian writers: Dostoevsky and Solzhenitsyn of course, but also lesser knowns like Turgenev and Lermontov. Then there was my educational, but at times, lonely year in Germany where, apart from attempting and failing miserably to tackle Herman Hesse and Goethe in the original German, I worked my way through the jolly scribblings of Maxim Gorky and Gogol.

On a lighter note I had enjoyed deliberately leaving my copies of various Henry Miller novels strategically placed

on the corner of my office desk so that my prudish
colleagues would stop, pick one up to look at the cover and
then mutter something along the lines of, *'Sexus'. Well I don't
know about that*. Having any of these books in my jacket
pocket didn't seem to impress girls much but it made the
interminable hours of commuting by train and tube at
least bearable. Having tried to find my soul through philosophy I embarked on a period of contemplation via travel
literature. I started with Eric Newby and escalated through
any number of other greater and lesser knowns. My main
area of literary geographical exploration centred on the
Indian sub-continent with occasional forays, if I liked a
particular writer's style, to other parts of the globe.

And of course I eventually read everything that Paul
Theroux produced. It took me a while to come around to
appreciating Theroux. On my first overland trip to India
someone had given me, or I had stolen, a copy of *The Great
Railway Bazaar*, by his own admission not the writer's best
book but probably his best known. In case you haven't read
it, it covers a trip the writer completed, mostly by train,
from London through Asia to Japan and back home. Set in
1975 he had been in many of the places I was travelling
through, indeed stayed in some of the same hotels, only a
few years previously. I was enjoying the book and Theroux's excellent description of towns and cities I had also
passed through until I reached the chapter on Afghanistan.

I had arrived in Herat, Afghanistan's third largest city
close to the Iranian border, a few days earlier. Back in the
late 70s it was still a beautiful, peaceful place. Elegantly
dressed women strolled through its quiet leafy streets and
the men, for the most part clad in thin suits or loose fitting
dark trousers and white cotton shirts, gave the appearance
of pride and love for their wild but beautiful country.
Tribesman were certainly around wearing their distinctive

baggy trousers and huge turbans but they did not seem threatening, simply bemused by the presence of us pale skinned westerners. The days of the Taliban were not far off but a naïve foreigner like myself, just passing through, could be forgiven for not knowing how much things were about to change. After an enjoyable but stressful few weeks in neighbouring Iran, where the seeds of revolution were far more advanced, arriving in Afghanistan seemed like a very positive thing.

Theroux felt otherwise as he attempted to cross the border, in the same way that I had, by bus from Mashad in Eastern Iran. *Afghanistan is a nuisance,* he wrote. This phrase stuck in my head for many years afterwards and when friends recommended one or another of his books I shied away not wanting to support such a heartless, thoughtless beast. Eventually of course I changed my mind. For him it was a nuisance as he wanted to complete his trip by train and Afghanistan had, and still has, no rail network at all. Theroux spent only a few days in Afghanistan, most of those simply trying to leave. I stayed longer and loved its wildness and its proud, friendly people.

But enough pondering, there were things to be done.

FINAL DEPARTURE AND A NEW
BEGINNING

L ooking back over the years I knew that there were a few things I wish I had done differently, projects not started and opportunities not taken. Who among us doesn't have these thoughts as they age? My list of regrets wasn't very long. It consisted mainly of places I could have experienced differently or more deeply such as not going to France when I had the chance at the age of 17. And spending more time in India, maybe even living and working there for a while. But in reality my life thus far has not been so bad. Long periods in Australia, France and Thailand plus shorter stints in Scandinavia and Germany. Definitely preferable, in my opinion, to staying in Herne Bay, London or Manchester. Side note: apologies to my childhood friends John and Neil.

As I locked the garage for the last time and headed back upstairs to an almost empty apartment I felt a pang or two of regret for leaving my life in France. True, the locals had on many occasions driven me crazy with their bizarre habits such as restaurants that only opened between the hours of 12:00 and 14:00 and again in the evening from 19:00; the feeling when you entered a shop that you were really disturbing the owner or staff from something else they would rather be doing; the driving style – only indicate when you are doing something you shouldn't. There were other less fleeting regrets, I was disappointed that my command of the French language had never risen beyond conversational and I never had done that bike trip along the Bordeaux canals or stayed in Paris for any length of time exploring all the places where Henry had lived.

But overall I'd been happy and enjoyed the beautiful scenery and fantastic climate of the Cote d'Azur.

Then I also remembered that I was heading for Australia via Thailand and somehow I knew the future would not be so bad.

REFERENCES

Milan, Kundera. *Immortality.* 1991.

Miller, Henry. *Tropic of Capricorn.* 1939.

Miller, Henry. *Plexus: The Rosy Crucifixion II.* 1953.

Theroux, Paul. *The Great Railway Bazaar: by Train Through Asia.* 1975.

Springsteen, Bruce. *Greetings from Asbury Park.* Columbia, 1973.

Springsteen, Bruce. *The Wild, the Innocent & the E Street Shuffle.* CBS/Sony Records, 1973.

THANKS FOR READING

I hope you enjoyed reading *My Brother's Bicycle* as much as I enjoyed writing it. Maybe it will inspire you to buy an electric bike or to re-live some of your own life journeys in other ways. I'd love to know what you thought of the book and hope you'll feel inspired to write a review on your favourite book publishing site. You can email me direct on ljstanley54@yahoo.com and sign up for more information about upcoming releases on lesstanley.com

ABOUT LES STANLEY

I'm a recently retired corporate citizen and haphazard blogger. Travel has always been a part of my life, either doing it or reading about it, and now writing about it.

I was, as Groucho Marx said, born at an early age, in London (England). My parents moved to the Kent coast when I was seven. I caught up with them a year or so later.

Printed in Great Britain
by Amazon